I'd Rather Be in Charge

I'd Rather Be in Charge

A Legendary Business Leader's
Roadmap for Achieving Pride,
Power, and Joy at Work

Charlotte Beers

 Vanguard Press
A Member of the Perseus Books Group

Published by Vanguard Press
A Member of the Perseus Books Group

Designed by Trish Wilkinson
Set in 11.5 point Goudy Old Style

Library of Congress Cataloging-in-Publication Data

Beers, Charlotte.
    I'd rather be in charge : a legendary business leader's roadmap for achieving pride, power and joy at work / Charlotte Beers.
        p.   cm.
    Includes bibliographical references and index.
    ISBN 978-1-59315-682-4 (hardcover : alk. paper) — ISBN 978-1-59315-692-3 (e-book : alk. paper) 1. Women executives. I. Title.
    HD6054.3.B44 2012
    658.4'09082—dc23   2011037222

Vanguard Press books are available at special discounts for bulk purchases in the U.S. by corporations, institutions, and other organizations. For more information, please contact the Special Markets Department at the Perseus Books Group, 2300 Chestnut Street, Suite 200, Philadelphia, PA 19103, or call (800) 810-4145, ext. 5000, or e-mail special.markets @perseusbooks.com.

10 9 8 7 6 5 4 3 2 1

To all the men and women who taught me that our work was always worth doing well and that there could be as much laughter in the halls as there was grief, sweat, and tears

What I do is me; for this I came.

—GERALD MANLEY HOPKINS

FRAMEWORK

INTRODUCTION

In my work life, I've held these titles:

Consumer research supervisor
Product manager
Management supervisor
Senior vice president
Senior partner
Chairman and chief executive officer
Undersecretary of state (I was "under" secretary of state Colin Powell.
They're very literal in government.)

Sometimes titles are not very descriptive. At one point in my career, friends changed my name from Charlotte to Shards (of glass), for breaking a number of glass ceilings. No one warned me that breaking glass ceilings meant standing in piles of broken glass, not upon a pedestal.

As a working woman, I've been called:

Our puppy
Flamboyant flirt
Scarlet
Chair chick
Very steel magnolia

Hurricane Charlotte
Charismatic chief

In 1996 I was on the cover of *Fortune magazine*, framed by a gigantic headline, "Women, Sex and Power." No wonder it was a best-selling issue. That's a triple power cocktail—women and power and sex. I knew and admired Pattie Sellars, the author of this groundbreaking article. Pattie passionately believes that women have a vital role to play in improving the workplace. But for this story, she got a little sensationalistic, pressing the people she interviewed about whether or not the star women she profiled, myself included, used their feminine wiles, good looks, or sexual fire to get an extra edge in the workplace. I wanted to kill her. We women had conquered vast, sometimes hostile territories at work with qualities like bravery, brains, and resilience, and I didn't want our accomplishments to be reduced to sex appeal.

In fact Ed Artzt, the chairman and CEO of Procter & Gamble, called me after being interviewed by Pattie. "Your friend Sellars called," he said roughly. "She asked me if you were sexy," he said.

I held my breath as Ed paused.

"I told her you are about as sexy as a Mack truck," he said.

I'll take the woman who delivers with the strength and drive of a truck any day over the one who is seen as flirting her way to the top. I wouldn't mind adding to my list of titles the descriptor "sexy as a Mack truck." Here's what I believe is sexy at work: being strong and committed and confident, being precisely who you are and in hot pursuit of the goals and ideas you believe in so much they captivate and inspire others.

I've now embarked on yet another career, one that all my working years have prepared me well for, and which I feel is a privilege. My new job description: teacher.

In these pages I distill all I've learned and witnessed—from my own career, from other powerful men and women, and from the many executive women I've worked with in my X Factor seminars—to show you how to discover your most effective, most powerful, most fulfilled working self. I want to show you how to lead, inspire, and influence others—maybe only one or two others, maybe hundreds or thousands or even millions. You can't accomplish this without knowing deeply the *authentic you* at work.

Authentic is not form. It's content. It's about the irrepressible power of being your largest, truest self. And it's something every leader has. If they were bells, they'd ring a true tone. They are completely who they are and sometimes even have to accept the consequences.

We women are not comfortable being "little men," and we don't like being boxed into what is considered womanly at the expense of being seen as leaderly. (I think I made that word up.)

And work is, finally, all about relationships: with ourselves, our peers, and our superiors.

I'd like to help you find your own unique, womanly way of leading. I'd like to put you in that sexy Mack truck that deposits you at a job that draws on all of you and allows you to show the world all that you can be.

I

PERSONAL

1

ENVIRONMENT

It's Not About the Work

THE END OF MEN, the magazine cover blared from the newsstand. It stopped me in my tracks. This was certainly a bold message that women are taking control of, well, almost everything. Of course I bought that August 2010 issue of the *Atlantic*.

This is a subject dear to my heart—the idea that women are winning, especially in the workplace. But having met recently with several male CEOs of marketing companies and just having dined with the head of J. Crew, also a man, I was pretty sure men are in little danger of becoming obsolete. And I don't know any working women who would want that to happen anyway. Most women would find a work landscape devoid of men to be a very dreary place. But we do want our fair share of the prizes and good positions. And one other thing . . . influence, more influence over our own progress and the decisions that shape our place of work.

As I read the article, reality raised its ugly head: "Near the top of the job pyramid, of course, the upward march of women stalls." That "of course" bothered me. Women are stalled on the way to the top. There is little evidence that the miserably small percentage of women who lead Fortune 500 companies—3 percent—is going to change soon. From the *Economist* (2010) comes this snapshot. "Women's rising aspirations have not been fulfilled. They have been encouraged to climb onto the occupational ladder only to discover the middle rungs are dominated by men and the upper rungs are out of reach." So, at the moment rumors of the inevitability of our running everything appear to be greatly exaggerated.

—⊗∞—

From Revolution to Evolution

Here's what I think: in our world today it's not that "men are so over," as a loud, red-suited woman declared to me at a cocktail party. But we women have won our revolution, and we are now on the cusp of a new era. Not long ago we had to prove every minute to every audience that we are worthy of working, able to take responsibility and generate results. That "prove it" phase has been replaced by a "forging ahead" environment. Women need not to be so grateful for every acknowledgment. It's time for us to let go of the sense that we are on probation and move on to take larger roles at work.

Women have made such progress that we can safely pronounce the revolution over. Some 51 percent of managerial and professional jobs go to women today, compared to only 25 percent in 1980. The drama of the revolution, when women pioneers were treated like celebrities or freaks, has been replaced by a blurry-edged evolution with little ceilings everywhere, not so high up but more opaque. One young woman law student was asked about these glass ceilings. She said, "Glass ceiling, you mean like a skylight?" She was blissfully unaware that while women make up 50 percent of graduates from law school, only a third of them have made it to even low-level positions of power in law firms.

This period of evolution has no clear rules or roles because our workplace is reinventing itself, and it is full of inconsistencies and misleading counsel for women. There is a lot of voiced support for women in almost every enterprise. Women are acknowledged as uniquely talented, are better educated than men (60 percent of all bachelor degrees go to women), and are very hardworking (give it to a woman if you want it done).

But this combination of a good education and hard work adds up to women frequently bearing the brunt of the workload but not being well represented in the tight circle of decision makers. That universe is still dominated by men.

One of our ceilings is that there is less real communication between men and women than we might expect. Women work easily with men side by side, but when women deal with authoritative and powerful male bosses, their sense of familiarity flees, replaced by undue caution and a wavering self-confidence.

It is so much easier to pick another fellow because he can be sized up much more reliably. It's not bias; it's more that "she's a mystery and she does things in a different way." Since picking the wrong people under you can capsize your career, men at the top who are making these choices would rather be right than fair.

> The men at the top aren't that great at properly assessing the women under them, certainly not enough to gauge their potential or intestinal fortitude.

Musical auditions are now often conducted behind a screen so the performance of the musicians can be judged on a gender-free basis. This little maneuver increased the number of women chosen by conductors at five times the earlier rate. But in most job situations, our notes are yet to be heard, our performance is in many ways an unknown. We don't have a gender-erasing screen. We have a ceiling.

A focus on political correctness has replaced frank and genuine work assessments with vague or coded reviews, opinions, and evaluations. Some bosses never dare to express what they really feel about a woman employee. The in-depth training that every company offers on how men should relate to women has greatly reduced and discouraged harassment, but in the process it has created a climate of caution.

For the life of you, you can't figure out how you are doing. Good luck getting a straight answer. People feel free to evaluate your work results but rarely give you an honest critique of your behavior. Men feel they have to be very careful about what they say and even how they hold their body when speaking to women. I'm not trying to romanticize the past, but it's unlikely a woman today will hear about her failings with the same candor I received coming up as a pioneering woman.

Discussions I've had with today's managers have taught me that a lot is being spoken in code. Once, at a closed meeting of top managers, I heard this report from Sally's boss: "Sally doesn't own her leadership."

What does that mean? I wondered. Did she lose it?

Nevertheless, the report had serious implications, because it implied that Sally would not be promoted to the next level. But Sally was not likely to hear this comment, so she'd never learn what she most needed to modify.

In evaluations, men have a built-in advantage because other men are more likely to speak directly to them: "Joe, don't be such a wuss! Answer back next time you're challenged—don't just sit on your tongue." Whack! That's how a guy will learn he "doesn't own his leadership." He gets immediate, unpleasant, and very useful feedback. Men still feel free to talk to other men, grab them by the collar, and give them a yank, usually in the right direction. This is the real-life version of mentoring, and it's far less likely to happen with a woman who is equally qualified.

During this cusp period, when women are evolving into these upper levels, there are two things that I urge women to accept and act upon:

- Women need to change how we see ourselves in the world of work.
- And we need to change the perceptions of those around us, to make our true potential more obvious.

Gathering ever greater influence starts with knowing your own potential. Obviously we can't count on others (read: men) to accurately assess our capability nor can we wait around to be applauded or recognized. This forging ahead period offers us an opportunity to gain more say in our workplace, affect outcomes, shape events rather than have them shape us. Focusing on titles and the career ladder alone won't get us there. What will is keeping alert for chances to speak up, to act, to be influential. We must be prepared to take controversial stands, initiate ideas and projects; that's how influence is felt. As we learn to be influential, the titles, recognition, and sense of accomplishment will follow. It doesn't really happen the other way around.

Once you refine your ability to understand what you want, identify what has meaning to you, and learn to trust your instincts and intuition, you will then need to master presenting these intangible and evocative but very influential aspects of who you are. And I don't mean the usual twenty power points presentation, with you obscured by the lights that are focused on the screen. I mean your presentation of yourself in persuasive and memorable ways.

> Every page in this book is dedicated to helping you know who you are and what you have to offer, so that your taking charge is what is inevitable about this evolutionary period.

Environmental Factors

The working women I've been teaching in the past four years have helped me identify the myths that need dispelling and the cruel realities we need to change. Through them I found proof that women are ready to forge ahead. They have helped me clarify my understanding of what it will take. I call these workshops The X Factor, referring to women's XX chromosomes. Men only have one X as in XY. That extra X is women's potential. It's the way women chose to work and lead. The irony is that in some ways it is harder for them (and for you) to discover the X factor than it was for me, one of the pioneers in the revolution. This is because of some interesting working conditions, in fact, three environmental factors.

Disconnect: Man to woman
Fog: The expectations laid on women
Filter: Accommodating, copying, hiding

Men Are Different, and It Matters

Many of the hostile or indifferent people who will greet you as you take on increasing responsibility and gather more influence are men. You may have worked with fellows all your life and think that you've got them figured out. But men are different to work with when you seek to be in charge, to take credit, to influence others. You will have to find a common vocabulary to communicate with the men who share important decisions with you or with bosses who direct your work life. You'll need to consider how men handle the competitive, politically driven situations that are part of the game; they know more about them than you do.

Men don't have it easy. They've got it simple.

As they're growing up, their parents, teachers, girlfriends, and neighbors make it clear that work is what their life is about, and that their successes will be celebrated: "Here's the ball, there's the goal. Go!"

Not all are quick or agile, but all are focused.

Our deep qualities and differing viewpoints have been a part of us from early childhood. A psychiatrist friend of mine once compared how six-year-old boys and six-year-old girls behave when they are introduced to a new friend. A girl's first question to the other girl is, "Who's your best friend?" The six-year-old boy asks, "How far can you pee?"

Men are clear about why they are working. They see it as a contest in which striving and competition are necessary and good. In my workshops, I always ask the women to write down what they see as the differences between men's and women's ways of working. Here's what they've zeroed in on, time after time.

— WAYS OF WORKING —

MEN	WOMEN
Vertical relationships	Horizontal relationships
What can you do to help me?	What can I do to help?
Can say no	Can't say no
Focused on tasks	Focus on interpersonal relations

— WAYS OF WORKING — (continued)

MEN	WOMEN
Competitive	Collaborative
Takes the lead	Workhorses
Speak out	Fear being labeled as "pushy"
Take risks	Use caution
Goal focused	Adaptable
Boasts about deeds	Modest
Self-feeding	Approval seeking
Less stressed	Less egotistical

You can appreciate that women are seen as more collaborative, more focused on connections, and more helpful, whereas men are seen as boastful, demanding, and competitive. Granted, there are exceptions to all generalizations, but they do dramatize how differently women and men are known to behave when there's more involved than just getting the job done.

These same descriptors have been offered by the women in every workshop, which means these differences are very real and reflect a disconnect. These typical male characteristics are a word picture of leadership, but as the workplace evolves, these attributes will be given a mighty shaking and reordering. For example, adaptability will come to have equal value to being single-minded toward a goal.

An important consequence of these radically different ways of working is that women need to speak and behave in ways that the men in command can understand. It may not be fair, but we can't wait for the world to interpret us properly; we will have to be the ones to find the common ground and the common vocabulary. Men used to compliment me by calling me tough. In other stories you'll learn the vocabulary men now use to describe desirable work qualities. One of

> When you interpret your actions or state your position to the men who are supervising you, it is not to copy, adapt, or manipulate them.

the qualities they frequently admire is "presence," remarking that a woman reporting to them needs more presence. Years ago I had to decipher what "tough" meant, and women today are going to have to parse out what "presence" means to the men they work with.

In bridging the gap between you and these men, you are acknowledging that they may be coming from a different vantage point. Several of these divergent male-female approaches show up most when a career move is contemplated.

Horizontal Versus Vertical

JCrew is a creative organization filled with talented, confident women at every level. When I was on the JCrew board, I asked to meet a sales team. Three women and one man gathered with me in the conference room. I felt a little sorry for the fellow. He seemed to be outmanned in competing with these obviously poised and confident women.

To get things going, I asked what they were each doing to get ahead at this hot retailer. Mia, wearing a sleek black sheath with her dark hair pulled back, spoke first, rather shyly: "I don't worry about getting ahead. I am concentrating on working very hard. I'm sure I will be recognized for that."

Susan, in a tailored gray suit, had an outgoing, almost cocky manner. "I've got a problem in a way. My customers like me so much they've made it clear they would hate for me to leave them, but," now her voice trailed off, "that's the only way up."

I wondered, Can these women hear themselves? I turned hopefully to Jessica. She was smiling. Her excitement at being in this company was contagious. She was a relative newcomer of only eight months. "I can't wait to meet Emily Woods, the daughter of JCrew's founder, who seems like she steps right out of the JCrew ads," she confided.

"But Emily is walking the halls here almost every day," I responded in surprise. I stopped. I realized she was not going to leap

out in the aisle and say, "Hi, Emily. I'm new and I love being here," which would, believe me, have earned her a big smile from that widely photographed face.

Matt, who had been waiting patiently, was ready for his turn. "Every time I give a presentation, I make sure to add in something that will reveal to the bosses, 'Here I am, ready for a step up,'" and he gave us a vivid example. There's no doubt about it; he's planning his next move and he's leaving nothing to chance.

If you look back at the list of male versus female descriptors, you see that a man like Matt tends to work vertically, keeping his focus upward. He is determined to demonstrate his accomplishments and his readiness to ascend. In contrast, women move horizontally, often waiting to be noticed or recognized for hard work, sometimes even willing to be locked in place by the approval and demands of their customers, giving the needs of others priority over their own progress.

Men also note these differences and are affected by them in significant ways, making assumptions about women's capacity and also how women should behave at work.

Fog: The Expectations Laid on Women

Men expect women coworkers to exhibit qualities they think of as "womanly." It gets really hazy when the situation is competitive and the issue is whether a woman is qualified to run the show.

Women are expected to behave in a more communal, kindly, and peacekeeping fashion than men are. These qualities are our inheritance, courtesy of our families, beaus, movies, myths, our own youthful fantasies, and the expectations of most of the men we work with. They are attractive characteristics: who wouldn't want to work with someone described as communal, collaborative, nice to others, and peacemaking?

> The womanly qualities we are supposed to feature at work are empathy, modesty, generosity, and selflessness.

These admirable characteristics may explain why your lover loves you or why you're proud of being a good parent. And there's no reason not to celebrate these qualities outside of the workplace. But these ways of working aren't good companions if, for example, empathy keeps you from making the right decision, or if being selfless translates to doing everyone else's work. Although such expectations may seem praiseworthy, they go a long way to keeping women out of the bigger, more authoritative arenas at work.

My smart, sophisticated financial investor friend Charles distressed me greatly when he went out of his way to tell me his women employees were the workhorses of his organization. Smiling as he anticipated my approval, he confided, "I fired all the guys; they were always messing around, asking for stock, pushing for rewards. The women just get the job done, never mind staying late, and are content." Charles looked at me, beaming as he described the happy workers who made up his very successful private financial firm.

My temper rose. "Well, Charles, you may appreciate women, but you're still making all the decisions and taking home all of the profits, aren't you?" I snapped.

There was a long silence. Poor Charles, I realized, was the wrong target. But what we women are being commended for is what keeps us in subordinate positions, and, as at Charles's company, not at all in charge.

These qualities, which we expect women to wear under their well tailored pantsuits, can morph into a readiness to copy others, a reluctance to express or even think about what they really want, or a failure to speak up and even to say (horrors!), "I deserve this." The way to evaluate these "womanly" descriptors is to ask yourself whether they are a deep part of who you are or whether you are yielding to expectations from others.

The former works because it's real; the latter is an artificial facade. The women in the workshops rate themselves from "Very" to "None" on such qualities, and the answers, as well as their rather heated reactions, were all over the map.

Katherine rated herself as "Very" on communal, selfless, empathetic, and nurturing because she considered those qualities an essential part of herself and her matriarchal family. Her mother and aunts ran the whole extended family. And Katherine had the most highly functioning and loyal creative team in her design firm.

But I pushed her further: "What happens when you need to step out, to lead the team; what do you care about, other than caring for others?"

Also on that list were other womanly habits such as "seeking approval" and "taking things personally," both of which work against us in the workplace.

Margaret resisted the idea that seeking approval is a problem. "I am much more motivated by someone giving me approval. It matters more to me than a new office, even money."

I agreed that approval is one of the rewards of working, but it's no substitute for having your own scorecard. It's good to enjoy applause, but not to need it. Someone else's estimate of you will not hold you steady. Your own self-esteem will.

As the women pressed me for how and when our womanly qualities become costly, I had to say, "I'd trade empathy for urging others to act. I'd trade being collaborative for the right to disagree."

> We must not sacrifice the bolder, bigger, braver sides of ourselves; we need to know when to choose leaderly over womanly.

Katherine is right to defend being empathetic and intuitive and taking it personally when she's coming up with a creative solution. But continuing to take things personally when she's defending that work undercuts her ability to take charge. Knowing when to shift from womanly to leaderly helps prepare us for gaining a larger sphere of influence.

No matter how grown up you are, how determined you are not to be womanly at the expense of being leaderly at work, the fog can slip up on you. Some aspects of being womanly are more detrimental than others. If you are focused on being communal, this can brand you as a great number 2, with a reputation for accommodation, a placating style of working.

The lure of being communal is that we wish all those around us were peacemakers and collaborators. But at work, such characteristics can be seen by a boss as: women are naturally peacemakers, which means they can be intimidated and they really don't like pushing back—they can't handle the lead.

And then there's modesty (that hangover from being grateful)—being selfless to a fault. It can cause you to start with and maintain lower expectations for yourself, and can cause you to fail to take the credit you've earned. I was lucky. I had a mentor to follow in my early career who wouldn't even consider not claiming credit for her work.

A WOMAN TAKES CREDIT

Marion was one of the few top creative stars at J. Walter Thompson in Chicago. She had a whiplash of a tongue that could make even the big boys tread lightly. During one meeting the account director was explaining to a client what we'd figured out about their product. "Our key insight . . . " he began.

Wham! A book slammed down on the table with a crash. "Was mine," Marion said coolly and finished describing the idea to the awed crowd. It was her work and now the whole room knew.

Afterward, the men on the account team, of which I was a junior member, were miffed. What nerve to hog all the credit. Later, when we were outside waiting to cross the street, some of the guys spotted Marion a few yards ahead. One of them leaned down and peered at her from behind, investigating something. "You see 'em?" he asked us.

"I think so, right there," said another guy, pointing with his chin. I knew this was for my benefit, but I wasn't sure why.

"See what?" I asked, taking the bait.

"Those balls hanging down beneath her skirt," they said, cracking up.

I felt my face burning and I wanted to kick them off the curb. They were making it clear to a young, vulnerable woman trainee that taking credit would earn you scorn and mockery. For some

*reason, I felt compelled to tell Marion about this episode. I imme-
diately regretted it as her face colored deeply. But then out came a
great laugh and then another. She was amused, delighted even.*

Let us all follow Marion's lead. When we feel diminished or are
called "pushy" for claiming our good work, we should lean back and
laugh. Marion laughed because she felt good about taking credit for
her own work when it was being hijacked. She called the gang on it,
and they felt challenged. So what? Marion was serving notice on them
not to try it again.

Autofilters: Self-Imposed Limitations

These filters are as subtle as the idea that we should behave in a womanly fashion. In fact more so, because they are our reaction to the
powerful fog men have created. We aid and abet their expectations by
setting up our own filter to automatically:

Accommodate
Copy
Fail to ask

That word "filter" cropped up when I was talking with Suze Orman, whose books and TV show on managing money have generated
a devoted and now well-informed following. Suze is a financial whiz
with the gift of making complex things understandable to the rest of
us. What's essential to Suze is to learn everything about an issue, strip
it down to the core truth of, say, how a certain mortgage works, and
then teach her followers how to be smart about something as emotional as money, investments, retirement . . . life.

A neighbor, who knew her only from her TV show, told me he
wasn't sure he liked Suze Orman. "Isn't she a bit abrasive?" he asked.

I laughed, "She's not just abrasive; she'll kill you if you do something stupid after she's shown you the way."

I was going to answer my neighbor more sharply, but then realized I didn't care if he understood Suze or not. She's an original, and authentically Suze. She hates it when people are foolish with their money. Millions of people love her tough love.

As a frequent guest on TV shows, even at the White House, Suze will not let the pressure of a situation or the awkwardness of a question throw her into hedging or saying less than the truth as she sees it. As she said to me, "Well, right or wrong, I have no filters."

It's not easy to become as authentic as Suze is, to work without a filter, without calculating, modifying, or adapting to all the expectations people lay on you. But it's the way to be more open and true.

Accommodate

When we're not sure of who we are and what we deserve, we're more vulnerable to taking the easy way out.

MARIE YIELDS

Women often wear a filter at work that screens out what's fierce and genuine in favor of qualities that get a stamp of approval from others.

When I was CEO of Ogilvy, Ford Motors was one of our big accounts. There was a drive for change and innovation at Ford, so I'd included our star, Marie, at a meeting where several other outside experts would also take part.

When I arrived, I saw Marie standing in the middle of the room with men from various other companies, most of them strangers jostling for position, waiting to get started. "I've been chosen to help everybody work together; they call me the peacemaker," Marie told me proudly.

"So who's the gloomy guy in the corner?" I asked her, nodding at a stern-faced man in a stiff blue suit sitting on the side, waiting for everyone to settle down.

"We picked him as the project leader," she said.

My heart sank. I could see what kind of man he was: controlling, more about getting the job done his way than leading everyone through the messy challenge of innovation. By the end of the meeting it was clear which of the two was the natural leader and had no fear of innovation: Marie. She had such low expectations for herself that she had agreed to play the support role.

The next day I grabbed Marie to show her how she had missed a precious moment to influence the group. And to lead. I saw the pain of recognition, then regret, play out on her face. She was furious when she realized how she'd been manipulated by their expectation that she'd make everyone happy, all with her complete cooperation. I assure you Marie will not be so quick the next time to screen out her natural ability to lead in order to keep the peace.

When we're not sure who we are, we're likely to borrow from someone else. Inevitably we are encouraged to become more like men. That doesn't really work. I know because I tried to manage like a man in my first big boss assignment.

Copy

I was the first female ever to be promoted to management supervisor at J. Walter Thompson Advertising. After I was offered the promotion, our office chief told me I was picked because as a female I'd be hard to miss and they felt the client would notice me and cut them some slack. Not a word about my previous successes or that I'd earned the promotion, or that they thought I'd be good in my new position.

I was in an overly grateful mode and meekly accepted his small idea of what I could offer. But I didn't believe that the fact that I was tall, Texan, and female was really going to impress Sears.

In the next six months, though, our team began to improve things with Sears, which I thought was a small step for all womankind as bosses. Then one evening John Furr, my best friend and in many ways my mentor, laughed as he casually told me that another management supervisor, Hal, had labeled my style of leading people as threatening. Hal said, "That girl manages by intimidation," John told me, still chuckling.

I gulped. This was hard to hear. The men around the office had nick-named me Scarlet, which fit perfectly with my idea of myself as a south-ern belle kind of boss. But then I remembered that Scarlett O'Hara was not exactly the most kind-hearted character in *Gone with the Wind*.

I began to watch myself, to observe my behavior with as much de-tachment as possible. And I saw that Hal was right. I often created false urgency, and I usually ended meetings on a kind of menacing note.

Who did this remind me of? My first boss, Morgan, from Uncle Ben's Rice. He was so brutal in dressing me down that he would make my friend at the next desk cry. He was urgent, demanding, and deeply in earnest. And now to cover up my anxiety about being promoted without any vote of confidence, I borrowed the toughest "I mean busi-ness" mask I could think of. I wasn't being myself. I was copying Mor-gan, all filters activated to screen out my own instincts. But thanks to Hal's timely critique, I rewrote my boss script, one meeting, one phone call at a time, shaping it step by step into my own style.

Fail to Ask

Failure to ask to advocate for yourself is another autofilter that has seri-ous long-term consequences. Asking for a promotion, a new position, a raise at work always feels awkward and is often actively discouraged by higher-ups. I can assure you that managers love a nonasker; it's simpler for them. So we women have agreed to step aside.

One of the most common justifications for not asking, going on auto-filter, is to take a position that you are above the fray. This means you'll be left out there on the ledge of your own making, too lofty to enter the competition.

The other autofilter to dodge asking is to deliberately stay below the radar. This is equally lethal to both men and women. It is the mistaken idea that you can avoid negative attention by hanging back without sacrificing your share of positive attention when the rewards are being passed out.

But the most insidious form of nonasking is "therefore" thinking:

> I didn't even get considered for that job;
> ### therefore
> I must not be good enough.

> I've done great work for four years with no raise;
> ### therefore
> My work and my effort are not all that important.

Rather than ask, pose a challenging inquiry, or find out what the prizes are and how we can earn one, we use "therefore" thinking, which helps furnish alibis for management's indifference.

> Powerful pressure is applied to make asking seem dangerous or ill advised, supported by our own autofilter tendency.

How to Clean Up the Environment

The long-term solution lies in cultivating a sense of self-esteem that enables you to develop world-class asking techniques: the very mission of this book. You can address both the elusive fog of expectations and your own set of autofilters by remembering to modify how you see yourself when you step out of the house on your way to work.

Here's a major bulletin: you are a different person at work than you are at home.

We need to sort out who we are at work versus who we are as parent, lover, or friend. At work we have special talents to put to use. We can test our boldness; we can measure our own self-worth. At work we need to focus on our bravery, resilience, and mental toughness. These qualities are as much our birthright as compassion and selflessness.

Yes, the world needs peacemakers and nurturers, and women are good at both roles. But at work you are not the peacekeeper. Nor are

you the PTA member. Look at it this way: work allows you to be someone totally different from who you are at home and in social situations.
It is liberating to have a whole new side of yourself to explore.

Allowing that work self to emerge takes practice. One of the
smartest and most accomplished women in our seminars, Gwen, got
uneasy when I asked her if she had taken credit for a big new idea she
initiated. "I don't believe in empty self-promotion," she rationalized.
But then she felt frustrated when others leaped up and took credit for
her idea. They weren't playing by her modest, self-effacing rules.

I'm not encouraging you to be a prima donna at work. When you
summon the strength to say, "I did this," it doesn't have to scorch the
earth around you. We each have to develop our own way of taking
credit that fits who we are.

> What do women
> want? Well, we
> want a seat at
> the table.

Another air cleaner is to think hard about what
motivates you. Nothing makes you more filter free
than being clear about what you want for yourself
at work. What men often want is to go vertical, up
the ladder. My classes with women suggest we
have a different way of looking at progress.

Women want to earn that place of influence in our own way. We
want to get the job done by forging such connections with others that
we create a community. Yes, we want to organize and orchestrate the
forces around us . . . BUT we want to be at the center.

Our Leaderly Qualities

Men have been trained to work with an organizational model copied
from the military, shaped like a pyramid, and top-down in style. This
system is still in place but it's outmoded, so men are having to learn a
new process that is more circular.

The very qualities that experts tell us will be necessary for companies to succeed in the global marketplace are the same qualities that
other experts tell us women have in great abundance. Enterprises of

the future are going to be more adaptable and flexible enough to change directions swiftly. They need to be able to see with a wider lens, rather than having a narrow, focused view of the products or services they provide. No one is going to make it alone. We must learn to be almost uncomfortably interdependent. The pyramid shape with the big boss at the top is being replaced by circles of creative teams, innovators, even artisans. Do these qualities sound familiar to you?

Women are born with a natural affinity for building connections, for communicating across boundaries. We have built-in verbal agility and we know how to hear what people mean, not just what they say. We're flexible in the face of wrenching change, and we're capable of being adaptable and calm in times of crisis and chaos.

Brain researchers have discovered that these coping skills are biological. Scientists now know that the area of the brain that responds when we seek connections with others is larger in women than in men. And they've learned that women have a sort of peripheral vision that takes in not only the person but all the surrounding information, whereas men tend to focus narrowly, reading a person from top to bottom. (That is why you've had the feeling that a man has undressed you top to bottom and you've only just been introduced.) By the way, this ability to focus so intently is why men are considered good problem solvers.

We also want a full partnership with men as peers . . . at the very least. What I've experienced when women move into partnership with men is that we all get smarter.

I recall waiting eagerly for a management team, John and Mary, to return from a meeting with an irate client so that we could plan our next steps. They reported as one unit. John said, "We know we can do these three things to answer his issues," and he gave a brief, smart summary. John stopped then and turned to Mary to speak.

"But I still think he is going to fire us," she said.

So now we had the whole picture. John focused in on what we could do to solve the immediate problem and he was right. Mary used her ability to see beyond the meeting and she was right. I felt we knew what to do. We could respond well to this client's frustrations, but we needed to also plan on replacing this business.

Women have that extra X, and as a result our brains respond differently to challenges. Being clear about the different ways men and women respond is priceless information, because it affects the way we communicate and deliver our work. It's a two-part reality:

- You are as smart and as capable as any man at getting good productive results.
- Your brain sends you down different pathways to get to the same goal.

Whether XX or XY, we have to understand and monitor our reactions at work. Men have far more brain space devoted to aggression, but they don't duke it out at the office. (Not usually, anyway.) Women have more brain centers devoted to connectivity, but they can't court friendship and approval at the expense of making good decisions or picking the best people. In fact I've seen more men than women cry at work, so we all get to violate our biological imperatives and expectations.

To Clear the Air, It's Not the Work

All of the people described here, the women in Charles's company, Marie in her big day at Ford, the very modern women at JCrew, are counting on their excellent work to speak for them, to win them more and more influence. What they usually gain is more and more work. If you always have your head down, buried in your work, a vital moment will be missed, a moment to lead. You can't afford to miss a single opportunity to step out and demonstrate your skills at leading.

That moment when you look up from your desk and take on a responsibility that goes beyond your various tasks does not always arrive with bells ringing. But when you step forward to demonstrate your potential, you do *not* let your work do all the talking.

In crossing the divide that separates even the world's best workers from those who want to be in charge, you will learn that two-thirds of your day is about delivery (the way you work), and about one-third is getting good work done well. Repeat this mantra every morning when you brush your teeth:

It's not about the work; it's how I deliver the work.

Delivery means the way you get your work in front of the right people. It's how you manage to get the work used properly and, drum roll please, "appreciated." That's the bare minimum you want from a good delivery system.

Your readiness to be in charge is all about delivery. Delivery encompasses how you let everyone around you know who you are—your gut reactions, your intuitive responses, what energizes you, what bores you to death. Delivery includes that moment when you've chosen to take a stand on something you believe in or a stand against a decision you think is wrong. It's easy to be lulled into thinking that the way you work is measured by the results, the numbers, the expanding business, *but an equally important measure* is how you behave, not just what you produce.

Have you caught on yet? The way you deliver the work comes from an interior place. You know all about the exterior you; it's right there on your résumé. But your delivery is about the essence of who you become when you're at work, your deepest, truest self sent out to play in the field of work.

Once you accept that the way you deliver the work affects your success, you will reorder your priorities like this:

- At times it's more about delivery than the work itself.
                    and
- I'm not the person at work I am at home.
                    and
- I'd rather be leaderly than womanly.
                    and
- It's my job to know and present my potential.

Warning: We're Not There Yet

It's in the nature of evolution that the old way is changing but the new way is not yet set; things are in flux. This is a perfect opportunity for women to get themselves ready to be in charge, to learn how to exert their influence.

Now is the time for us to prepare to stand out as managers, leaders, and influencers.

You women who are working right now are the solution.

You are far better educated than other generations; you are acquiring more expertise every day and now you need to develop forging-ahead skills; to be prepared to forfeit popularity and pleasing others in favor of tough decisions. You can handle dissent or even hostility because you know yourself and you've developed superior communication skills.

These are qualities you must have because the new, more circular organizational systems, which reward innovation and adaptability and are so friendly to a woman's way of working, are not yet in place. The men are still at the top running things, peering down in consternation at the women reaching out in great numbers toward them. We can't wait for company structures to change; that's too slow. We know better than to count on men adapting to fit our way of working. Instead, women can learn to stand up and say, "Choose me" or "I'll do it."

We all have larger dreams than being known as the hardest, most competent worker, though every success starts here. We dream of recognition for work well done, a chance to contribute in a big way, moments of taking the lead and truly being ourselves in a way we'll never experience outside of work.

This quote from Johann Wolfgang von Goethe is perfect for our era.

"Talent is born in solitude, but character is formed in the midst of men."

Learning who you are at work, getting a grip on the size and shape of yourself in the midst of men *and* women, is a great opportunity to explore and perfect your character. You can refine and perfect your *ability* to do the work all by yourself, but you can only enact your largest self when you mix it up with all the wonderful, curious, and exasperating people at work.

Together we are now preparing to take the next step, to embark on the journey to know who you really are, to sweep away other people's expectations and directions, and to honor your own, so you can rise up; one small ceiling after another.

A Story: Internal Affairs

The oldest, most enduring form of teaching is storytelling. The lessons slip in on the wings of a plot, through a variety of characters, a colorful dilemma, and, finally, a solution. Stories reveal lessons that can't be reduced to rules and charts.

A strange thing happened to me when I left the huge, sophisticated J. Walter Thompson advertising agency for a new job at the midsized Chicago ad agency, Tatham. I began waking up at 4:00 AM every morning, my heart drumming, my otherwise orderly brain running one disaster scenario after another. In the daytime, my panic at what I had tumbled into at Tatham was suppressed, but at night, it rose up to convince me I had an unsolvable situation. For the first time in my work life, I had hit a wall.

I'd had every chance to try on my manager's hat at Thompson, but it seemed to come at too big a price. I had become the first female senior vice president in Thompson's ninety-nine-year history (J. Walter Thompson moves slowly, its wonders to perform). I was among two or three contenders to become general manager of JWT Chicago, which would have made me head of the third largest office in the JWT worldwide empire. But for reasons I couldn't completely nail down, I felt uneasy at the prospect. Some instinct warned me that life would be very different if I jumped from mastering the work I loved to managing the whole agency, dealing with profits, liaising with other offices, headquarter trips, forecasts, and so on.

As I looked through this big glass ceiling, I realized I didn't know what general managers did. They seemed so withdrawn, so worried, so enmeshed in the many layers of Thompson's vast ruling class, and yet I'd been taught to aspire to this next step called management.

I did know if I took that next big step at Thompson, there would be a lot more "first woman" press. That spotlight would not enhance my home life. Unlike the men who were also contenders, I had to factor in the very real tension I was experiencing between home life and work life. People had already asked my husband if his wife made more money than he did. We had no experience in functioning as a two-worker family in which the wife was the "star." My husband, seeing me so immersed in work, felt he was losing me to an unworthy competitor.

So I accepted an offer from Tatham to become the new CEO, but I insisted on having a year of preparation as a senior partner. Tatham was an agency for companies like Procter & Gamble, Ralston Purina, and Miles Laboratories. The clients were as big and as smart as those at Thompson, but the office was smaller, the press attention less relentless, and there'd be no pressure from corporate headquarters. Most interesting of all, the Tatham partners owned the agency. I could become a real manager without sabotaging work challenges . . . or my marriage.

Then I learned that sedate Tatham was not an agency with a "few problems" as I'd been briefed, but one on the brink of ruin. And it wasn't sedate, either. It was like a B movie featuring booze, drugs, and wanton women.

The problems were bigger and more gut-wrenching than anything Thompson could have thrown my way. I left my first big manager's meeting with a sinking heart and a headache the size of Alaska.

When our financial officer in that first meeting talked about "broadies," I thought he must be talking about bonds; but no, this was his word for Tatham women. Ugh. He laughed slyly about keeping "two sets of books." An alarm sounded. Did he mean fraud? No one in the room was laughing at the growing mountain of debt as clients left or cut their ad budgets. Then I had a realization that felt like an electric shock. Given the way the partnership was structured, the owners, myself included, were personally liable for company debt. If someone sued us, they could take our homes, our investments, my daughter's bicycle.

Clearly all of the managers had lived with two sets of books and had accepted this kind of looming liability. But it made me feel sick, as if we were already listed in the lost column.

When the meeting broke up, a mystery woman appeared at lunch and, judging from the nudges and winks, she was someone's good "friend." What have you done? I asked myself on the drive home. Really Charlotte, what have you done?

My growing uneasiness about our finances had to be hidden from the few teams who were ready to dig in and rebuild Tatham. Still, as we reviewed budgets, the big office rents, the unproductive payroll, and the clients who were late in paying, I had to concentrate hard to keep my voice from shaking.

I knew my reaction was not the norm; the people around me didn't seem to share my high anxiety. Thompson was a big company of deep pockets, so financial issues had never come up. It wasn't just the thinness of our defenses at Tatham. There was a radically different culture and I had to fit into that culture . . . or change it. Part of it was a freewheeling attitude toward alcohol and drugs. It was quite different from the drinks at lunch ritual, widely considered a necessary treat in the ad business. I watched in amazement as our creative teams left at 4:00 PM to drink in the local bar, led by none other than our chairman.

In my first months, we managed to find some relief. I led the new business pitch for Korbel Champagne and we won. That steadied my nerves and my belief that we could rebuild. But only six months later we lost the account. The reason? Our creative team was caught smoking pot in the company guesthouse at the Korbel Vineyard. As it turned out, our client was also the local sheriff.

I had about as calm a reaction to the distinctive fumes permeating our halls, the pot smoke and booze, as I did to the idea of a spiraling debt load. Both made me dizzy with worry; how could I even begin to confront such wrong-minded ways of working? I was plagued by an unfamiliar sensation—a sense that things were out of control. We had team problems, morale problems, doubting clients, and what seemed to be a financial quagmire. And now, I had to add, perhaps the wrong CEO successor: me. I didn't recognize this troubled and frightened version of myself.

I assumed, coming over from J. Walter Thompson, that I was locked and loaded for success because I had a proven track record at all aspects of client service in advertising. My confidence had been tested many times before: I'd learned to cope with bosses who diminished me, good friends who quit speaking to me once I was promoted past them. I'd even dealt with a client proudly showing me his pornography collection. But the situation at Tatham was crippling me, and I had to figure out why.

Whether I liked it or not, I was about to meet the "stranger within," the interior self I'd been avoiding for years. Part of the reason work was so important to me was that I could use my brain, my energy, my problem-solving skills; those parts of myself not called on as much in my roles as mother and wife. I believed that the workplace was about performance, which was a welcome change from all those less tangible and more emotional forms of connecting, with family, friends, beaus, and children in my home life.

Now I was discovering that work included sleepless nights, anger, chest-clutching anxiety, frustration, and fears that didn't fade at the end of the workday. I never would have thought that my chummy, good-natured, and respectful relationships at work could be matched by troublesome, disturbing, even scary ones. And it was becoming clear to me that a lot of this was my personal problem. I was slated to be the one in charge, yet I was more frozen by the situation than any of my colleagues seemed to be. Pondering this bleak reality, I sat late in my posh corner office looking out on glittering Michigan Avenue, a place I had once yearned for. Now it all seemed grim and hopeless, and I could see no way out.

And then, in the nick of time, only two months before I was due to take the reins as CEO, a way out appeared in the form of a job offer from another big, successful Chicago ad agency. Ah, escape. I could taste the relief, the kind that comes from waking to find it was all only a bad dream. I was rehearsing my departure speech when I was stopped cold by a single word. The word was "fearless." And that word was how one of my senior colleagues described me.

A few weeks before, the top people at the agency had participated in anonymous reviews, giving us an opportunity to be thoughtful and honest about one another. The first review I turned over read, "Charlotte is fearless." I was stunned. "This has to be a mistake," I muttered to myself. Reading on, I found other, equally unexpected descriptors that elaborated on this quality; words like "brave" and "decisive." Who in the world did they think I was?

It was hard to reconcile this huge gap between my personal crisis of confidence and my coworkers' descriptions of me as some kind of office warrior. I sat with that for a while, trying not to judge either perspective, looking at myself from their side and from my side, pushing my anxieties and insecurities aside. I had been quick to move against the entrenched bad habits at Tatham, and even quicker to support the brave and true people who kept the firm going. I had kept good people from leaving because they believed in me and our hopes for the future.

Slowly, like a compass shifting a few degrees to true north, I began to see myself in a new light. With some distance from my disabling thoughts, I was able to see this troubled ad agency from a more optimistic vantage point. Maybe disaster was not our destiny after all. Maybe I actually had been given a chance to help create a whole new agency. I'd gotten so caught up in the company's problems that I couldn't see my own potential, or Tatham's for that matter.

I was surprised that no one had noticed how stricken I was by doubt and uncertainty. Maybe what they saw on the outside was a promise of what also lay inside. That was an energizing idea. I began to pursue the question of where something as powerful as "fearlessness" came from. "If I'm so fearless," I said to myself, "then why am I paralyzed by things that others seem to take in stride, like our debt or the wild ones in the agency?" Clearly I was being driven by strong emotions and deep instincts that were not consciously known to me. I knew right then I needed to understand what they were and where they came from.

I didn't leave Tatham. Instead, I began to discover Charlotte—to find out who I was from the inside out, from the center. We all have a deep desire to discover our whole self, but we can set up very sturdy barriers to avoid doing just that. Demanding, engrossing work can distract us for a time but not forever. When the world moves you into a new sphere where relationships are front and center, that relationship with yourself becomes the first priority.

For the ten years I was CEO of Tatham, I had two jobs: managing Tatham and discovering what qualities within me were reacting, doing the driving, creating the anxiety, stoking the bravery. To do so, I had to become a keen observer of myself in relationship with others.

My great chum Bill Ross, a creative director, once told me that he was keeping a journal. "Oh, are you going to write a book? I asked. "No," he answered slowly, "I want to see who I'm becoming."

I too began to keep a journal. By paying attention to cues and signals, I learned to notice how my behavior affected me and others. In these stories I found many clues about what matters most to me, and I began to see when I was running against my beliefs or my truest instincts. I also became aware when I was being a jerk. I recorded the qualities of people I admired, such as my secretary, Vasso, whose sheer tenacity was legendary, and the junior high girls from Cabrini Green (a soulless housing project that has since been torn down) whom I tutored in the evening. I taught them reading and they taught me another face of fearlessness and dedication. Those twelve-year-old girls got up every single day intending to do their best in the face of many disadvantages they could not change.

I learned that I brought to work a bag of mixed messages drawn from my family and the behavior models I had copied. What are these doing at work? They aren't on your résumé, but they do get a daily voice in your delivery of the work. Once I began to connect my puzzling reactions at work to early influences, I made real progress. Our family was damaged in a way that only alcoholism can cause. My reaction to the drugs and drinks at the agency was to feel as helpless as I had as a child. But in many alcoholic families the children also grow up early and find a bravery that is essential for their survival. As I looked at my past, I understood how I came to embody both fear and fearlessness in my approach to work.

The turmoil at Tatham activated another unanalyzed problem: my nearly pathological dread of debt, something I learned from our volatile family finances. Old wishes surfaced too. I had always longed for a more perfect family, so the partnership at Tatham, more like a family than a traditional company structure, was a powerful attraction to me. These contradictory responses added fuel to my uncertainty about who I was and what I could really offer as Tatham's CEO.

Although I traced the way I chose to behave at work directly to family inheritances, I also discovered I had my own unique way of delivering the work. This was a real eye-opener for me. It explained why every problem client at Thompson had been handed off to me. I got a lot of applause when we turned around yet another disgruntled client. I felt like the Statue of Liberty: "Bring me your tired, your broken, your clients yearning to be free." The truth is, I had asked for these broken businesses. I gravitated to trouble, wanted to lead the cavalry. When I accepted and understood that better, it helped me to chart my career deliberately instead of inadvertently.

This inherent trait was another dimension of fearlessness—an instinctual desire to be in charge. When I tracked the source of this instinct, what I found was not always attractive, but at least now I knew. There's a great freedom to knowing who you are in that inner chamber because such knowing is the source of self-confidence.

As I was growing into the role of manager and sometimes lonely leader of Tatham, my personal transformation was keeping pace, though less publicly. I attended Adult Children of Alcoholics meetings, and in telling my own stories, I heard how oversensitive I was to hot debates, which recalled earlier scenes at home that could escalate to violence. But I was in a company that desperately needed to debate its future and not always politely. Another contradiction for me to sort out.

I longed for the old days at JWT when I knew exactly how to orchestrate our talented teams to get the ads out. But I knew I couldn't continue to swallow my fear and uncertainty every day without destroying myself, and Tatham along with me. I had to learn how to manage it. Through diligent exploration, through my journals and research, I found my own system of self-discovery and correction.

I gathered strength from the fact that the people at Tatham thought I could lead us out of the mire, even while I was engaging in a lot of interior hand-wringing. I was still living with a sometimes confusing split in my personality: my bold career woman's role and this corrosive self-doubt churning inside. But the more I learned about myself, the less disruptive the churning became.

A hardy band formed at Tatham, and we began to use the fact that we were smaller than our competitors as an advantage: we were lean, flexible, and fast. We presented a David versus Goliath story, since the giant agencies were always slower to respond. I brought dazzling women into every agency department, making Tatham the first agency to do so. We began to improve the agency's image, much as I had reset my own role.

Our work and our teams, our ads and out thinking, improved so much we hit a winning streak. In some six years, we had won big new brands from Procter & Gamble and Ralston Purina and added Oscar Meyer and Nabisco. For our people, the apex was a profile of Tatham in the New York Times as the fastest-growing agency in the United States with record profits.

I began to practice for myself what we used every day in making ads, promotions, strategies . . . all the disciplines and secrets of communicating. Communication is not just delivering information, which is where most people start and stop. It is about persuading, inspiring, and presenting. My job now demanded these higher forms of relating to others. When to stand, when to fold, when to jump, were judgment calls I had to learn to make. Agency people have a world-class education in how to communicate, how to find the one right strategic solution, but we have a lousy record at applying it for ourselves. I didn't have a choice. We could not buy time for Tatham if I didn't try on more innovative ways of presenting myself and our future.

I tell the story of what I learned about myself at Tatham to make a point about the power of self-knowledge. We all face, from time to time, a situation gone wrong, but I'm hoping you can read between the lines that the big leap for me was identifying and making friends with my whole self, including that potent inner chamber from which instructions are also issued, day after workday.

Watching yourself closely and objectively is not easy, but it's good for everyone around you. Self-knowledge means you can act with more consistency. You can offer trust. You can say what you mean. There's no substitute for a deep, honest study of who you are, beyond your title and job description. Having a clear sense of who you are and all that you have to offer is the foundation of true self-esteem.

You can take this journey in a more reasonable manner than I took mine. It breaks naturally into two frontiers:

To know yourself.

To acquire the tools you need to present that self.

Although this system of self-inquiry made a huge difference to me, I wouldn't be offering it to you if I hadn't received plenty of confirmation from the women in my workshops that this process gave them a larger view of themselves and that the presentation skills they acquired gave them a more effective means to "show" that self in their work lives.

Here's how they put it:

- *The impact of this training has been enormous. It has allowed me to understand early influences and how those experiences contribute and/or* become barriers in my leadership. Having that awareness helps me use my new presentation tools with courage. I even let the passion out. I've learned to spot the defining moments and approach tricky business situations with eagerness, not fear.

- A continual self-auditing of my behaviors, a greater self-awareness, and a sense that I need to watch for old ingrained negative habits. I practice my presentation tools in every point of contact. People look amazed; it's fun.

- I think the piece that has stuck with me most is that once you master your trade, there are so many other aspects to being successful in a more senior role. Before X Factor, I believed that if I was a master at my trade then everything else would fall into place. I learned there is so much more to it, particularly what I personally bring to my role. I already see an impact.

- A new belief that I am worth a lot to this organization, and the courage to speak on my own behalf with senior management.

- I took on the office bully, the one I catered to; chewed him up like chocolate.

And one frequent response I didn't expect, but love:

- I have a much keener interest in championing the cause of women generally. I am much more aware of the need to advocate for women in my department, and to encourage them to "to get out in front of the work."

Are you ready? Please take up your own journal. What will be written there will be more important as what is written here.

2

MESSAGES

How You Learned to Engage

GWEN WAS A rising star in her public relations company. The only thing that could derail her fast track to the top was her reaction to the increasingly complex personal situations she faced as a newly anointed manager of their biggest account. Since everyone rated Gwen as the best thinker and the most innovative problem solver in her company, this wasn't about the work.

Before Gwen became a top manager, she enjoyed a much higher comfort level. She said her clients compared her to a Volvo: "I crash through walls to get the job done and my passengers arrive safely." When she made it to the management level, everyone tugged at her sleeves. Clients called night and day, the creative boutique threw one tantrum after another, the CEO wanted her to demand a higher fee, and, the last straw, her reliable partner quit. Her job wasn't simply solving work problems anymore. It was about managing relationships and she felt pulled apart by jealousies, arguments, and competition issues. Most of all, she didn't like the glare of an unrelenting spotlight.

Her CEO was rethinking her appointment: "We're all wondering which Gwen will show up. One minute she's excited, inspiring us, never giving up. Then comes this darkly pessimistic and withdrawn Gwen. Where does that come from? Who is the real Gwen?"

During a particularly stressful time with a demanding client, it was Gwen who gave the writing team an idea for a TV special that would allow the client a forum for pet energy issues. Then she nursed the idea to fruition. The boisterous lead writer took over the big presentation, and as Gwen watched from the sidelines, it turned out his was the only name mentioned in the film credits.

You met Gwen earlier. She was the one who said she didn't "believe in empty self-promotion." Now she was fuming openly about not getting any credit for this work. "I am torn by ambivalence. I can work furiously, but then I pull back, literally walk away. I feel like there are vampires around sucking the life out of me. Success has a dangerous quality about it."

For such a brainy, cool, confident person, Gwen didn't know a lot: like whether she wanted to succeed (how much of me will it take?), or why she wanted to walk away from certain situations, or what made her so shaky under the bigger spotlight. And yet she was exhilarated by the thrill of getting her ideas and solutions launched. Gwen was so frustrated and puzzled that she was willing to stop and investigate. Why did she have such an uneven and unpredictable way of handling the relationships that came with being in charge?

Gwen accepts that she is the one who is sabotaging how she delivers her work. She has an outward self-confidence, but her self-esteem, that private conversation she has with herself, is eroding daily. She is trying to take on a leadership role without something essential to pulling that off. She doesn't know where her reactions and impulses are coming from or how to reroute them.

Getting to Know You

There have been many studies on what makes leaders successful. One camp believes successful leaders have a collection of qualities such as charisma, inspirational ability, and emotional intelligence. An-

other camp believes that a leader must embody humbleness, diffi-
dence, and an ability to be relentless. Notice that first-rate work performance is assumed.

Though such qualities may be desirable in any given situation, I
think the studies are missing the point: what a leader needs first and
foremost is self-knowledge. What Gwen needs to create a more effective delivery system for that big brain of hers is a far deeper understanding of herself, which will give her confidence in who she is, not just in
what she can do. The authentic Gwen will know how to manage herself and recognize how to respond when she engages with others.

Gwen has one great advantage over Eleana, a department head in
an accounting firm: Gwen is acutely aware that she's relating to others
in a disruptive, self-defeating way. Eleana doesn't even know she's not
engaging well, but her boss knows.

Eleana was asked to cut costs in her department by 10 percent. She
did a good job of finding the least harmful way to eliminate projects
and people. When she chose how to tell people they had to go, she was
making a delivery decision. Her choices were to deliver the painful
news in person, to delegate it to someone else, or send the news via a
memo. Eleana decided to delegate this painful assignment to someone
else. Her boss gave me this critique: "Eleana always manages to leave
town when there's something difficult to do or there are tough decisions to enforce." The key word there is "always." He feels this is an essential pattern of how Eleana engages with others
and it's hurting her.

The choice you make on how to handle a
complex personal engagement sends a message
about who you are. There are many ways you can
respond when you're told to cut costs: you may be
fearful (this could happen to me), angry, determined to protect the best people, discouraged, or
resilient in adversity. Because it's exhausting to
fashion a new response to every different experience at work, all of us develop a regular delivery

Unless you want
unseen hands
moving you
around like a
chess piece at
work, you need
to define the
essential nature
of how you
relate to others.

system, a default approach to challenging situations. The question is, Do you know how you deliver?

Eleana's biggest problem is that her boss knows her delivery system better than she does. Eleana does not think of herself as a dodger, but as an optimist, a builder of happy teams.

Outdated models and harmful messages from others that aggravate Gwen's ambivalence or activate Eleana's tendency to dodge trouble can be replaced with new, affirming models and messages. Models like Emily Brontë, who wrote, "I'll walk where my own nature would be leading. It vexes me to choose another guide." It vexes me too; no one is better qualified to guide you than your own interior self. "Guiding" in the form of aptitude tests, mentoring programs, and coaching is already a huge business, but every one of those programs will ask you to first answer this question: Who are you?

Your Inheritance

Part of how you see yourself at work reaches way back to influences from your early family history. We are taught how to behave. We develop responses that become reactions—outward expressions of those early family messages. We also learn by watching others handle various interactions, and those lessons about how to cope become deeply embedded in us.

Work wakes up yet another side of you, calling up different responses, reactions, and coping techniques and puts them out there for everyone to see. It's more than how you perform the work. It's the way you offer the work—in meetings, memos, conversations, presentations. Who you are, not just what you do, is front and center.

The stories of Gwen, the ambivalent star who hates the limelight, and Eleana, who avoids trouble, demonstrate that we will have to deliberately decide how we want to engage others at work as we take on higher levels of managing. What training can you call on to do a good job of firing people or of taking the lead, dealing with animosity and dissension along the way? There's no manual to follow. You're going to have to reset how you respond in these more intensely personal kinds of engagement.

Our first training in people management comes from our families. We learned what responses were approved, and we developed actions and reactions. We watched and molded our own behavior. Much of what you learned then comes with you to work today.

If your present response to a challenge is based on behavior you learned from others, then these outside influences are calling the shots. Some messages we received from our families are inspiring and have become an important part of who we are. Other influences are negative or disempowering or simply a bad fit for your life at work. The point is that to know who *you* are, you need to look deeply at these early influences and choose what to keep and what to jettison.

Your Inner Critic

We women tend to judge ourselves harshly when we don't have an accurate understanding of how strong we really are. In private moments or on entry questionnaires for workshops, even the most successful, confident women will reveal they feel "not smart enough," "weak," "boring," "inadequate," "vacuous," or "an imposter." These negative tapes running inside, which one woman labeled "my inner critic," take over when there's no counterpoint from our bigger, truer voice. "I simply had no idea these brilliant and composed women we are hoping will move up to the top positions feel so vulnerable," a human resources head for one of the companies sponsoring an executive woman's seminar told me.

We're vulnerable because early on we're given false pictures of how women should behave. And because the models are usually men, we have little insight into how to engage when we want to take the lead. That means we work removed from our familiar state and strengths. We often don't realize this until a crisis hits. Then we have no choice but to strip ourselves down to discover not only who we are but why we respond the way we do. If you can locate and look at the influences that have shaped you and shed the ones that are obsolete or destructive, it will make any crisis to come—and there will definitely be more than one—easier to manage. This also helps muffle that noisy inner critic.

We're also vulnerable because as we move up the ladder, many of us carry a view of our workplace as a "safe" house, a place run by rules, logic, and predictability. For many years, I viewed work as an escape from the emotional, messy problems I encountered elsewhere. I wanted to solve marketing issues with nice clean products that didn't talk back or wander off to bars in the middle of a crisis, as the creative did at Tatham.

Here's what women say about working:

"Work is as important to me as breathing, a place to breathe and to be safe."

"I work to keep my sanity. It's a calmer, satisfying part of my life."

"I work to get out of my own head."

"Work is my hiding place, an escape from the other; it's my drug."

But as Gwen and Eleana discovered, work can't keep its promise of being sane and safe and calm. Every opportunity, every new frontier calls for a different and deeper level of engagement. Your best defense, your ability to jump into the fray well equipped and eager, is to know yourself and what you can offer.

Connect Who You Are With Work

Not everyone wants to know what their work can teach them about who they are. I was having lunch with a woman who owns a spa and a man who is a successful financier. I was describing to them my discovery that we need to know why we interact the way we do at work, and my system to track this. The woman started taking notes furiously. I was so excited about her enthusiasm that it took me a while to notice that our financier had moved so far away he was practically sitting at the next table. I had to say, "Bill, please come back. I'll stop talking about getting to know yourself."

That scene still makes me smile, but I did learn he was quite in-triguel. He asked me later if I was still working on my "IQ" questions, the "introspection questions," as he called them. Then he one-upped me. He asked if I'd do a workshop for his key men and women. "After all," he said, "this idea is not just for women, is it?" A very high IQ, Bill.

Bill (and you) will be glad to know that there is a shortcut: a series of well-tested questions that guide you to distinguish your true nature from all the adaptations you've made on how to behave at work.

These family influences can be relentless forces throughout our lives, some for better; others for worse. Whether or not you're aware of them, they play a big role at work. Often they show up to sabotage us. Sometimes they are the source of great advantages.

> A large part of how I responded to others, especially in a crisis, was learned or assimilated from early family influences.

You receive information all the time at work about how your early message system is leading you to behave, but it's up to you to connect the dots between you and your work.

In my early days as CEO at Tatham, Joe, our account director, took me aside and said, "You know, you never let us finish a debate. The minute a voice is raised, a chair scraped back, a thump on the table, you move to shut off the dialogue. We need to work out these issues; they're not going away."

I had been ricocheting between being fearful one day and fearless the next, and I knew there were family influences that had triggered this inconsistency. Arguments at home could escalate from anger to a threat of violence, and those experiences were dictating how I reacted to loud voices and the threat of angry action at the office. That was a connector of the dots for me.

Where do we learn to engage with others? At our mother's knee, drinking in the messages delivered as direct instruction ("never rely on a man") as well as the oblique instructions we take in as we watch how she shows anger, competitiveness, and appreciation, as she expresses values and laments unfulfilled dreams. We don't necessarily obey and may vow not to follow (I will never be like my mother). We internalize messages and models from other members of the family as well, about what's valuable, how to view winning, how to judge ourselves.

Some of these old messages can create a level of constant self-criticism. In order to move freely and without doubt, we have to step back. We have to revisit the family voices, the people, and the environments that shaped us. It's a difficult job, and even sophisticated therapists tread carefully. But we have a shortcut and you will have some partners in your journey back to the family messages.

There is a system I used to learn how to drill down to the essential patterns of how I related to others at Tatham, when all of a sudden I was thrown into top management. I didn't have years to spend diagnosing my problem and neither do you. It has to work as you are working "in the midst of men," as Goethe says.

The women who attended the workshops where we tested this system for several years were all strengthened by this self-scrutiny. They explored the myths, biases, admonitions, and mottos that came from family, friends, and neighborhoods, any environment that can be a factor. My state, for example, was important for me because Texas is a place that seems to say, "Think you're big enough? . . . Give it a try."

Dare to Open Pandora's Box

Many of the subterranean messages we women receive encourage us to be guarded about ourselves, especially at work, like keeping a "stiff upper lip," a style that shows no emotion and allows no cracks in our surface poise to reveal what's churning inside. We need a new model to begin this study of the self. I chose Pandora because she had the temerity to open a forbidden container that threatened to let loose unpredictable and disruptive forces, over which she eventually prevailed. It takes courage to lift that lid on the Pandora's Box of your family influences, but there's treasure to be found there too.

Pandora is often called the "first woman" in Greek legend. I love her stubborn curiosity. She was explicitly instructed not to open the beautiful box another god had given her, but she did it anyway. Who wants a gift that cannot be opened? Maybe we working women are all guilty of not opening our gifts, hidden as we are behind our work, befogged by other people's expectations of us and assiduously applying filters that screen out our genuine selves.

When Pandora opened her box, sorrow and turmoil were let loose on her world. In particular, one was "no longer can men loll around all day; they have to go to work." No more lolling, fellows, and it's all our fault. But Pandora survived these tribulations and found a treasure at the bottom of the box: hope; it was also referred to "a larger set of expectations."

Zeus conceived Pandora as a snare to men, a creature with a beguiling and graceful exterior who was intended to house a deceitful nature and crafty way with words. But Pandora didn't cooperate.

Pandora is a wonderful inspiration for us because she wasn't afraid of what she would find when she opened her box. She refused to follow the gods' ill-intentioned instructions to stay dumb, and rejected her assigned role of being nothing but a tricky snare—more womanly than leaderly.

> A larger set of expectations will emerge if we dare to open Pandora's Box to find layer after layer of interpretations and warnings given us by the gods of our impressionable childhood—our parents, siblings, and extended families.

Each of us sets off every day for work with our own Pandora's Box strapped to our back. Open the lid and many troublesome memories and disturbing visions may fly out, along with wicked messages and models potent enough to affect you in your work life. Fortunately, you'll also find joyful reminders of triumphs and inspirational moments.

Your task is to sift through these influences, mend some, strengthen others, and discard a few. At the bottom of the box, you too will find a particular treasure, a sparkling gem whose clarity reveals what parts of you are truly yours, and what parts were imposed by others and may need reassessing. I promise this clarity will give you a larger set of expectations for yourself, a firmer understanding of who you are, and a stronger ability to realize your full potential.

How does opening up to family influences apply to work? Many of the messages you find in your box will be about parenthood, marriage, or life itself. The women in the workshops easily distinguished which voices and scenes specifically connected to their life at work. Not only that, they were able to see the consequences of those messages:

	Message	Reaction	Work Effect
Ida	We didn't fit in; as immigrants, my parents were so naïve.	Have to watch others closely, to adapt.	Never the insider. Work from outer rim.
Pauline	My coach said I swam far better in practice than in trials.	I'm not good at direct competition.	Now I'm stuck on a second tier.
Lydia	Don't get caught in drama.	Keep head down.	Cool, unapproachable.

As you recall family tales, recognize messages, and reinterpret moments, your understanding of how these affect your workday will shift. You may get off to a few false starts, but eventually an interesting and very clear picture will emerge.

The Five Key Questions

On the way to that clearer picture, there are five questions which will help you separate your true nature from all those potent messengers:

1. What did your mother say?
2. How did your siblings affect you?
3. How would you describe your family life?

4. What was most significant about your family?

5. What gifts were you given?

These were the questions I used to reach a more objective self-assessment in a time of crisis. I can guarantee that if you start right now, wherever you are on your work map, the answers to these questions will give you a sense of how to be in charge of the one person for whom you are responsible . . . yourself.

In your answers, you will begin to uncover the influences that dictate so much of how you engage at work. How long will this take? A lifetime. But you start learning from day one. Uncovering the influences that these questions reveal will change your work life forever, and for the better.

It's self-directed. You're the only one who can initiate it, and the most important tool you can bring to this inquiry is your own close attention to how you work.

This is not a study in how remarkable you are; rather, it is objective scrutiny. Ideally, you can find a buddy to act as a sounding board, to keep you from making up alibis or missing a clue. Someone to help you put things in perspective. Someone who "knew you when" is a good choice for a buddy or someone who gets the environment you're in. A department head in a medical university sought out a woman who was not a close friend but also held a position in a hospital because the world of men and women in medicine is so full of taboos and secret handshakes that she needed an insider.

> Learn to become your own watcher so that you are interested and perceptive but not biased or judgmental.

As you answer the questions and jumbled memories surface, focus on how the messages (some of which are negative and judgmental) affect your way or working. Here are two guidelines:

- Leave out all the factors that affect your life as a mother, daughter, friend, and lover. You will quickly connect how certain messages particularly affect your life at work.

- Try to answer the questions in order. They will unfold more naturally that way, since each question prepares you for the next.

1. What did your mother say?

Question 1 takes the lid off the box of early lessons because there's usually a lightning bolt kind of instruction we remember vividly. Perhaps your father gave you a way of viewing work, but your mother is there in the background, a dominant factor in how you engage with others and how you view your role at work.

My mother said, "Remember, you can only go as far as your husband." This was electrifying to me, and I remember answering in my head, "I don't think so." It was a powerful incentive for me to resolve to earn my own way. These larger-than-life creatures, our parents, can instruct by their actions, without saying a thing.

Rachel was distressed when her mother married her divorce attorney only weeks after her divorce. To her mother, safety was a man. Rachel remembers thinking, "Mother, can't you ever be alone, on your own?" As a result, Rachel was determined to never rely exclusively on a man and she hasn't. In fact, she's been the primary breadwinner throughout her nine-year marriage, and sometimes she regrets it.

- Mothers can be negative about work:
  "All your father does is work; that's no life."
  "It's more important for your brothers to go to college; they're going to work."
  "Remember that family is more important than a job."

- Or they can be motivational . . . and threatening:
  "Don't sit around and wait for some guy to come along."
  "Take responsibility for your own happiness and support."
  "You figure it out; it's your career."

- Some are frankly disempowering:
  "Why do you want to struggle about evaluations? Relax."
  "All that really matters is your reputation."

Messages from your mother can have a long life, affecting how you see yourself at work. Megan's mother said, "I know you'll be happier if you stay home and have a family like I did." To Megan, this message was dishonest since her mother was the bitterest person she knew. Her brothers seemed to have a totally different mother; they were encouraged to go out and conquer. Megan was told to stay home. Megan left home at sixteen and earned her own college scholarship. She describes how she works as intense but also defensive because she feels she always has to prove she's worthy of the job.

One of the most pervasive influences our parents pass along is their own unfinished business and unrealized work dreams:

"Do anything, but be happy." (From a father who hated his work.)
"You'll only be happy working for yourself."
"All my hopes and dreams are in you."
"I did all this so you can succeed."
"I missed the brass ring in this business, but you can grab it!"

This last one was the message Paul received from his father. The business was advertising, and he was raised on a steady diet of the heroes of advertising, the ad campaigns, the glamour of it all.

I met Paul when I had just become CEO of Tatham. Paul was completely out of place at an ad agency. He was rigid to a fault, miserable in the face of change (our daily task was to adjust, refine, and improve ideas for demanding clients; it required real adaptability), and hidebound. He tried to solve everything with charts, complex agendas, and order. That was Paul's delivery system and it didn't work in an agency full of cynical, irreverent people. Paul worked harder than most because for him, his job was a daily adjustment to a land where he didn't speak the language. I realized he had to go, but it was misery. Here was a man who worked hard and cared deeply.

My voice was unsteady as I told him that he had the wrong way of getting work through the agency. Plus, he was not able to motivate people to join in. Though he kept perfectly still, a tear slipped quietly from the edge of his eye. He ignored the tear, but as I watched it hit his collar, I wanted to take every word back, to find some way to make it work. He startled me when he finally did speak. "My father's dream has just died."

His father? There it was; the unfinished business, the message to Paul: "A career in the ad biz, now that would be a great achievement."

> We're susceptible to someone else's idea of good work when we have never teased out our own deepest wishes and affinities.

In the end, being fired liberated Paul. Rudely stripped of his father's directive, he was left to form his own ideas. He built a smartly tailored, buttoned-up coupon redemption company that focused on order, accountability, and numbers. It became a big success. It was a complete match to his way of engaging in people and work. He was a new man, deeply absorbed in work that satisfied him. And he probably didn't mind at all that he made more money than most of us at the agency.

2. WHAT DID YOUR SIBLINGS TEACH YOU?

Brothers or sisters or cousins, even best friends, give us our first practice at dealing with peers and engaging with the opposite sex. The messages that siblings give are more glancing than the frontal assaults from parents. But they are potent, nonetheless. When we hang out with our siblings, we practice how to compete, we see what's valued, who is cherished and why.

- Siblings Define Our Role
  "My sister got all the attention. She was supposed to bring us fame, but she opted out: no college, menial work. I became the backup career girl."

- Siblings Become Parents

  "Basically, I was the protector of four other kids. My parents were busy having breakdowns. I took that caregiver role right into work."

- A Closed Circle

  "We were so close in age to our parents. We raised each other and did everything as a unit. I'm pretty isolated at work."

  "We had a huge extended family. No one was left out or unprotected. I'm a 'mom' at work too."

KAREN'S SISTER

Karen's way of competing with others was directly related to her sister. Her belief was, "Winning is not worth the grief." She was struggling because she'd recently been pitted in competition for the general manager's job. In the seminar, all were horrified to realize that she felt it "wasn't nice" to try to beat someone out for a promotion. Karen was able to trace the reason for her fallback style to her sister, who was very important to Karen. Her sister was the beauty in the family, treasured by all.

Karen, who felt like "a potato" in comparison, early on decided to shine in other ways. Since she was the brainy one, she excelled at all levels of study. That was never as valued in her family as her sister's grace and looks. Her parents suggested she put too much focus on achieving. She ended up feeling guilty for making her adored sister feel inferior, even dumb. Now, when she's faced with direct competition at the office, her first response is to step aside.

Back Against the Wall Club

From my siblings, I learned to go for freedom, what bravery looks like, how to handle rough male teasing. It was great survival training for entering a man's world.

My two brothers and my little sister, ten years younger, taught me many things, like the sweet comfort of loyalty when our family was in one of its regular crises. But the big lesson that affected my decision to work when no other girls in Texas were even considering it came when I was just six. I saw clearly that my brothers and their friends, the boys, had much more freedom than girls. They had freedom to choose how to live and freedom to earn their own independence. I vowed to enter their world. I was the only girl in my advanced math and physics classes. I had to prove I could think like a man.

I wasn't treated gently. My brothers teased me so continuously that I had to learn how to handle it or live in perpetual tears. When I entered my first "all boys" kingdom at J. Walter Thompson, I could take the rough teasing in stride and the guys knew it. I'd been well trained at home.

But the biggest message I absorbed was what bravery looks like. My brothers were physically brave, with strong characters. Ralph Joe, my older brother, was a first-rate boxer, even though he wasn't a big guy. Glen Edward, who was closer to my age, ran away from home over and over and survived many lickings. Both Ralph Joe and Glen Edward showed me that bravery was necessary and wouldn't kill you. Clearly, though, I had to find my own form of bravery.

Our turbulent household forced us to grow up too soon. I considered us to be charter members of a club I privately named the Back-Against-the-Wall Club. We had been put through survival training in our volatile, sometimes frightening home life, so we developed a kind of mental resilience. My two brothers and I became top managers in our work life. I think we wanted to exert some control over people and events, but I also think we were less respectful of the dangers. In interviewing, evaluating, and promoting people, I could usually recognize members of this club, and I must admit I favored them.

When I was searching for the source of the "fearlessness" that my fellow workers at Tatham recognized, I traced it to this combination of influences. (The fear came from elsewhere.)

3. How would you describe your family?

This question is a warm-up for the next one about your family's significance to your work. My students took this as an opportunity to make a summary picture of their family they've been holding all along. These brief family descriptors that came readily to mind were directly connected to how they deliver the work:

	My family	Delivery style
Sam	A clan: tightly knit, superior.	I don't engage much.
Rachel	Constant battles. I'm always mediating	Let's all be friends.
Alice	None of us succeed if one of us fails.	Success in group.

My family history translated to a dual personality:

Charlotte	"Not normal."	Fearful and fearless.

This question about the family in total invites you to step back from the influence of any one individual and regard the family as a whole, to consciously recognize the core family dynamic. When we considered these overall family descriptors, the women in the workshops began to gain a real context for seeing how they operate at work.

There were strong cultural imperatives from the family:

- "My family is from a foreign culture. They did not know how to fit in. Their naïveté hurt me, left me open to being ridiculed. The result is I'm very vigilant about my company's culture. I know the hidden rules."
- "We are Irish. We work hard. It's honorable to work and it's great if you can help others. I do not make compromises of my integrity for work."

Family as maverick:

- "My family is eccentric. Education was not as important as experience, so we moved constantly. Though I was at the top of my class, I quit math. I have a degree in microbiology, but I'm in the creative department. I jump around a lot and get bored easily at work."

My family is everything I don't want to be:

- In every group I worked with, there was at least one woman who did not want to be contaminated by things she didn't like or identify with in her family. This influence makes for a strong allegiance to a career and a powerful determination to succeed. Such women are described as driven, wanting work to be their home in the world.

Not Normal Families

I characterized my family as "not normal," but that was before I realized how few normal families there are. Since I felt I had never experienced a happy, loving family, I converted my company into an extended family. Over our gradually successful years at Tatham, my favorite chums, my brothers and sisters in arms, left Thompson to become partners with us at Tatham. It was a golden time, with young women in every department to celebrate and applaud. Our top management was bonded by deep friendship and respect.

Can you see the problem coming? I couldn't. I had created the loving, secure, not overly intimate family I had always longed for. Eventually we hit a slump and I was powerless to act against my adopted family. Others saw it too. Could you fire or demote your sister or uncle? Neither could I, and the agency was on the verge of stagnating.

I came up with a solution. I was the one, the head of the family, who had to go. The ad world was surprised, to say the least, to hear that the pioneering female CEO was going to step down at the peak of her success. I had set a trap for us all by creating a culture of personal loyalty and friendship, making emotional well-being more important than results and the right teams. When I left, I vowed never again to attempt the lovely fiction of making the office my family.

4. What is most significant about your family?

The first three questions are preparation for this one. The answer to this question cracks you open to reveal the core issue among the many influences in your professional life. You focus on how your family history affects how you behave at work. As our women faced this question, they made their greatest progress in connecting who they are with how they learned to engage at work.

Alice, a new manager at her company, found that this question revealed issues critical to how she handled her new job. After answering the four questions, Alice felt her way of working was to give up too much of herself. Her first overly negative take on her delivery system was that she behaved at work as though everyone else owned her. She had claimed no place of her own. Her mother had always emphasized the look of things, and reputation rated above all. She and her brother took music and dance lessons and put on performances, though Alice was very shy. Alice's answers to what was significant about her family provoked her into wondering if she'd ever thought of herself as an individual because the family message was one for all, and all for one:

> The most significant thing about my family is they were haunted by the memory of *their* families being dangerously poor; only if they hung in together would they survive. Today that's not the case at all, but my family is still living, and urging us to live, the Three Musketeers' motto: All for one.

Alice really can't accept that role for herself. She's the new manager of the Detroit office, so someone must think she can handle being out front on her own.

Margo's family's most significant directive was, Life is not fair.

The most significant, the inescapable reality of my family was that my brother was sick, so sick it diverted all of the attention, the money, and the happiness from my other brother and me. My mother was right when she said "life is not fair," but I can see it has carried over into my work, so that I believe I should never strive to go first. And that's not fair! Just give me a chance and I'll find the number two spot, rather than number one. I see now I have a rocky road ahead because I've trained my bosses to see me as the most useful thing, a great second lieutenant.

My Family

The significant factor surrounding my family was that my father was a dedicated alcoholic. Our lives were shot through with turbulence, uncertainty, and dread. The days passed in seemingly normal fashion, but the nights would explode with potentially dangerous confrontations. My father's personality changed when he had too much to drink, and my mother was then roused to fury.

My father, a gifted oil man, would do well for a while and then be demoted or put on probation due to his drinking. When that happened, we would be filled with uncertainty about money, safety, and family stability. My mother then had to take menial jobs she disliked. She was a frustrated scholar and felt demeaned by what she saw as sideline work. Her frustration was a daily lesson for me about self-sufficiency. I became a "pioneering" woman because I never believed in marriage as a means to security. In my earlier working days, I ranked self-sufficiency way ahead of partnership with a man.

Traveling back to my childhood and listening to the experiences of other children of alcoholics helped me understand why circumstances at Tatham were so deeply frightening to me. My fear of our family falling apart was real. And I had transposed that fear onto my position as CEO of Tatham. That vivid memory caused me to exaggerate the threat of Tatham's financial liability. I had become the small child again whose reaction to insecurity at home was to lose my breath in asthma attacks. When I finally recognized that my anxiety was an extension of how I had once responded at home, I was able to begin to step away from that fear.

"After all, I have a degree in math. I can figure this out," I admonished myself. When I mustered the nerve, I dug in on the financial statements and realized we had options, we were legal, and we had some time.

All children from dysfunctional families have a heightened sense of anticipation. We must be vigilant. We are always scanning the skies for what will go wrong, hoping, of course, to head it off. That ability to look ahead, to anticipate, was a great advantage for me, not only in the advertising business but also with our clients as I spotted trends, got ahead of their needs, and smelled trouble in time to squelch it.

> Accepting that we can all be both fearful and brave, and that we've acquired all kinds of coping skills, is not a bad inheritance . . . unless we let it speak *for* us.

Once you observe these influences and trace the origins of how some of your behavior came to be, you are ready to review the gifts you received from your family.

The Healing Question

5. WHAT ARE THE GIFTS YOU WERE GIVEN?

During my own self-study, I attended a two-day symposium at the C. G. Jung Institute in New York City. I will always remember how Harry Fogarty, a renowned psychiatrist and theologian, opened the meeting. He simply asked, "What were you given?"

This question offers us a great way to heal after the tumult of the first four questions. It allows us to step back and see how our early influences, our family, and our environment sent us into work armed with special talents, potent drives, and redeeming characteristics.

The signature grace of a family gift is that we don't have to do anything to earn it. We don't have to refine it or unwrap it. It's just there.

In one of my European workshops, a woman who built a specialty marketing company in Russia described her family's influences in a way inspiring to us all. She told us her mother, father, and aunt all left Russia and moved cold turkey to the United States, so that she could have a good education. That's a message of being personally valued, a message that says you have an important brain the world needs.

Our Parents Give Both Milk and Honey

My family's gift to us children showed itself in a type of confidence that became obvious when my two older brothers and I hit the worlds of engineering and business, and succeeded on many levels. Given our family circumstances, this strong sense of self-worth was an unexpected gift.

We puzzled over how this could be. All of us shared a belief that we could handle anything that work, or even life, brought our way. None of us could remember any occasion or messages from our parents that deliberately instilled self-confidence in us, but we all seemed to have it.

> Milk is a mother's unconditional love, while honey is self-worth and optimism about life, transferred by a kind of osmosis from parent to child.

When I read Erich Fromm's *The Art of Loving*, the puzzle was solved. Fromm characterized the gifts parents can bestow as either milk or honey. And some lucky children get both. Either way, it can't be taught or delivered in behavior or words.

My brothers and I and our much adored younger sister had all received this honey, which seemed to travel like mead from the hearts of our fractured parents to nourish us.

My mother, on the other hand, did not give me that unconditional love, the milk. She was too distracted at times to even see me. But one day she sent a look like a laser that went right through me and said, "Anyone can get married. What are you going to do?"

It didn't do much to improve my view of marriage, but clearly she felt I had important things to do. Thanks, Mom.

Gwen Gets Some Answers

Gwen, mentioned above, had a delivery system that was overwhelmed by a lethal ambivalence. She was a woman with more questions than answers. She got some important answers by looking at early influences and messages.

Here's what Gwen said about her mother: "I feel I'm entering the narcissist's lair when I think about my mother." One big message from her mother was, "Go get it for yourself. No man will ever bail you out."

Her mother was a striver—a lawyer for thirty years. From this, Gwen soaked up the message that work is fulfillment. Her father was an inventor. He never patented an invention, but he could fix or devise anything. He wanted her to use her brain, her inventiveness. However, her father was not a wage earner, so her mother made it clear that she should rely on no one except herself.

Siblings

Gwen had two older brothers who never gave her the feeling they liked her. It's hard to deflect such a message, which was never voiced out loud. But they did speak up when they began to feel the threat of Gwen's powerful intellect. They told her she was greedy, full of herself, way too ambitious. "You're not as hot as you think you are."

This is where her mother complicated things. Instead of defending Gwen and encouraging her achievements, she warned her, "Throttle back. People will hate you if you're successful." Yet another time, this willful woman told Gwen, "Marry rich. It's easier."

Family

Gwen described her family as both amazing and terrible. The significance of her family was this barrage of mixed messages. There was dysfunction, addiction, striving, and brainy standards, which all added up to a generally threatening environment.

It's hard to imagine a better recipe for being ambivalent at work. Eventually Gwen began to understand her tendency to withdraw at work after a joyful thrust of energy and success because any dislike or envy from others would cause her to freeze in her tracks. Gwen began working to overcome these imposed messages: "I am going to have to risk the spotlight. My brothers aren't even watching anymore." But she still has questions. "How much of me is it going to cost to succeed?"

Gifts

An answer emerged as Gwen pondered her family gifts. "I learned I am as dedicated a striver as my mother; I need to accept that. I quit work for one year, but I was miserable. I have to find a way to strive, to create, and contribute without these meltdowns."

You've Got Some Answers. Now What?

At first, it's unsettling to question old "truths" and to try to erase false pictures we built up to defend against the many voices we remember from childhood. Here's what you can do:

Shed
Amend
Magnify

You retain and react to many messages because they are (after all these years) still in your Pandora's Box.

Shed: Some messages are simply not worth keeping. It's not about shooting the messenger, because sometimes you are the one who kept a deadly influence polished and shiny, using it for all the wrong reasons. Pauline was the swimmer, and she hung on to her coach's critique of her poor showing at swim trials well past its "use by" date because it was a handy crutch to use to make her feel she was above the highly competitive games at her real estate broker's office.

Amend: What I heard from the workshop women as they assessed their findings was phrases like "I don't need that anymore" or "That was important when I was twelve," and "I can see my family as people now." And this one: "My parents were so hysterical that I marry well, I viewed my work as a means to find a man, but no more!"

Magnify: To discover you have wonderful, intrinsic ways that deserve polishing and expanding is nothing less than transforming. Every one of us has personal ways of being that lie dormant and voiceless but deserve to be activated. The women's faces shone when they spoke about clearing away old dreary practices to realize they can be resolute, imaginative, and strong in adversity.

When Megan casually told us that she left home at sixteen, won a scholarship, and attained success at her law firm, we were thunderstruck at her sheer resilience in the face of a family who told her to stay home. When she walked back through that history, Megan saw that she was a gutsy woman who never gave up on herself. That's a self-image worth magnifying.

How It Feels to Answer the Five Questions

- "It's beyond the intellectual, so that's the trick. My family has done therapy for years. I always avoided it, but this is mind-opening, refreshing. It's like winging it, get the answers to these questions down and then start to figure it out every day at the office."

- "To me, the next steps are built in. We sort out how this stuff affects our daily work and then there's an opportunity to consider changing it."
- "I don't feel I'm wallowing in anything. It's an objective study of a subjective issue and I have somewhere to go with it."

The excavation, as our women not so fondly called this self-scrutiny, revealed some issues that needed further examination:

- Sam says, "It seems I prefer not to engage much."
- Rachel adds, "I move too often to be the peacemaker."
- Alice is troubled. "I give myself away to every request, every needy person."

In applying this same system I had to develop at Tatham I learned a lot about myself, but I still didn't know where that label "fearless" came from. I had to continue my "excavation."

The next dig is from deeper within; where you will discover you are the director in your very own private stage play.

3

TRAITS

The Stranger Within

TRAITS ARE THE interior drivers that run your work life. They are powerful inclinations that may not show up as you are getting an education or early in your career. These big engines will come roaring out when the going gets serious, when you're being tested.

If you think about the key players you know well at work, you can readily identify what seems to be their abiding trait, rather like spotting their primary source of fuel. I've worked with Martha Stewart long enough to think I know one of her primary traits. I've witnessed her cookbook, *Entertaining*, become the foundation for a magazine, *Martha Stewart Living*, and then that magazine become a multimedia group that now includes magazines, TV shows, and products for the home, garden, and pets. I think Martha's most fundamental trait is "I want to know more." She has a powerful ongoing curiosity about how things work, how gardens grow, how fabrics perform, as well as the whole complex chemistry and taste of food.

Martha is admired by friends and coworkers for her limitless energy. When she wakes at 4:00 AM, needing less sleep than normal mortals, she watches mathematics classes on TV. I think it's her deep and respectful curiosity about the way the world works and her willingness to be a fresh student every day that is the source of her powerful energy.

One morning, when I was staying in her guest cottage, she came over as I was slaughtering a mango, trying to get to the fruit. She took it from my dripping hands and, never once interrupting her conversation, with two deft knife moves, laid the meaty thing open, perfectly ready for eating. That's Martha. In case you've ever wondered, she *really can* do it all herself: reglaze windows, assemble a fabulous cherry pie in ten minutes, and build a world-class compost heap. All three of these wildly different projects requiring totally different skills were featured on the first TV pilot she planned to submit to the networks. When she showed it to us, she couldn't understand our amazed laughter. "Is it enough?" she asked. The only problem with that sample TV show was that the TV moguls could not believe one person could do all those things . . . equally well. But they were willing to learn, as her TV audiences have been learning ever since her first show taught us all how to give honor and care to the daily tasks of our lives

---

The Inner Chamber

Becoming acquainted with your own deep drivers, those instinctive reactions you bring to the people and circumstances at work, is another essential aspect of self-knowledge. Traits are different from family messages because they are from within.

> It's exhilarating to be able to name the central drivers that affect you so much at work.

The family messages and models that shaped and influenced us, which we discovered in our Pandora's Box, are external, though we absorb them and they show up as part of our delivery system. Your instinctive reactions to the various experiences at work come from your inner chamber. They're not going anywhere because they live within you. But they can be channeled, unless, of course, you don't even know they exist, which is a serious form of impoverishment.

Think of these driving forces as the great river from which your strengths and weaknesses flow. Anyone can recite outward strengths to a prospective employer, such as "I never quit until it's done." Don't you want to know where that inherent tenacity comes from? Sam described her weakness as "I just shut down when there's a lot of conflict around." But that quality is only a clue, a symptom of a deep, instinctive reaction. This is something Sam needs to understand because "shutting down" is not high on the list of desired attributes in managers.

We are each wondrously fitted with qualities so strong, so abiding that they *will* drive the way we work. These need to be distinguished from the strengths and weaknesses that you identify in evaluations, training courses, and job interviews. If you are rated a great collaborator, that ability to bring projects and people together is driven by an underlying trait. Finding traits is layered; it's an interior excavation.

An out-of-control trait is a dangerous thing at work. Randolph's dominant trait at work was to foment: to create drama and disruption, to stir up speculation and intrigue in the absence of a real issue. He was a senior officer at J. Walter Thompson when I was a junior, and he was awesome. He came to Chicago from London because of his skills as an internationalist. In fact, he lasted only a year. After meetings I would see him whispering in the corridors, which turned out to be his favored delivery venue. He'd interpret situations or make veiled accusations that confused people and created uneasiness. In spite of his keen knowledge of Europe and Asia, and his deep understanding of his client, Kraft, he could not resist making the simple contorted, nor could he do without the thrill of manipulating events and people. Unable to gain people's

> Inherent traits are powerful, perennial, and unavoidable.

trust or respect, he couldn't survive. "All that talent" his colleagues would say, shaking their heads, when he left Thompson. Randolph's instinctive and out-of-control need to make trouble, to foment, overwhelmed his other impressive qualities.

If you don't get to know these traits, they'll master you rather than the other way around. When you identify, understand, and harness them, you locate the source of your personal power.

Begin by Spotting a Trait in Someone Else

It's not hard to identify other people's key traits because their instinctive reactions occur over and over, and we can observe what sets them off, as well as what they react to with zest, with determination, or perhaps avoidance, even fear.

I was having lunch with a headhunter, a fellow who had placed many a CEO candidate, especially in the financial investment field. We were talking about these desirable inherent traits (as I defined them) in Wall Street whiz kids. He said they considered fear an important motivator. He felt being driven by a fear of failure was a great goad to a ceaseless kind of circling of what's good, what's next, what's wrong. That type of driving trait might be destructive in another situation, but "fear of" is where a lot of people begin when they describe an inner drive they've observed in someone they work with.

Velma had a strong impression of her boss Ham's dominant trait:

> My boss is a very senior fellow who always takes care to maintain his altitude, a view from the top. But his energy is neutral—he has no curiosity or interest in any subject . . . (already we don't like him). Though the more I think about this, the more I feel compassion for him because I realize he's afraid. The reason he never dialogues, never debates, is *because* he is afraid we will find out he has nothing to contribute, doesn't know what he's talking about. Aha! It's not that he doesn't care! It's fear.

It's much easier, and more fun, to search for a significant trait in someone you deal with at work than to look for your own, but you'll notice how such drives tend to affect everything they do at work.

My creative head, Thomas, is a complete hedonist, and he's totally guilt-free about it. It makes him a very efficient manager because he doesn't waste a moment on anything that does not add to his own pleasure. But you would never call on him in a crisis, because he's not going to work late or go the extra mile; it's not worth it to him. It's a good thing that when he's on, he's brilliant, because he's too self-centered to be part of a team.

Lisa wants to rewire her boss's trait:

The woman who runs our department is a control freak. The upper guys think she's great because she's aware of every detail. It's actually toxic because nothing is good enough until she redoes it. The simplest things are complicated just so she can save the day.

I think her underlying drive is that she doesn't understand anything unless she can go through it herself, from soup to nuts. I'm going to get her a helicopter so she can learn to do a flyover.

Maybe management does see the downside of this trait, because she just got rejected as a candidate to move up and I know it's because she gets totally lost in redoing everything.

These drives are so fundamental that they issue daily instructions on how you should react, but the traits from the fomenter, high-altitude flyer, hedonist, or control freak are not dependent on male or female characteristics. They're more like fingerprints, unique and gender neutral.

> Traits are gender neutral.

Finding Your Own Trait

The easy way to begin your own traits search is to recall moments or actions when your deep instinctive responses seemed to telegraph exactly who you are. At this stage you are looking for clues or stories that are typical of you and reveal distinctive behavior.

It's important not to focus on how wonderful you are; this is not a job interview. It's a search for the "real."

Trait Clues

GWEN: "I have always been able to 'read' people. In my company, they call me the 'good witch.'"

PAULINE: "I'm a driver. I drove sixteen hours nonstop; never gave my husband the wheel. I *cannot* be a passenger."

RACHEL: "I hate the phone; I think emails are phony, inauthentic. I want to look people in the eye. It saves time and I don't trust any other way."

Pauline is not sure where or why she's driving, but she has to take the wheel. Rachel's first clue is "I rely on my instincts and I don't like to engage unless I can see for myself." Gwen has to think about why she's the "good witch." It's such a specific identity.

As they initially attempt to identify their own traits rather than someone else's, the women in the workshops resort to generic words or relist strengths they have been told they have. Gwen's first traitlike label is "I am intuitive." But when she explores examples of how this operates at work, she recalls situations that tell another story. "You are like a turtle without its shell," her partner told a depressed Gwen, who felt completely emptied out after a two-day conference with IBM.

Now the trait is further defined into something more true and specific to her: "I realize I am acutely sensitive." Gwen takes in way too much and has no barriers against what the crowd is saying or thinking or demanding: "I almost die of sensory overload."

Gwen's "good witch" behavior, being acutely aware, is her instinctive response when being pushed and pulled by ambitious, intelligent people on opposite sides of the complex issues her public relations business faces. Unfiltered sensory overload almost sent Gwen on emergency leave; in fact, she did drop out for a year. Gwen needs to protect herself from taking in everything that comes her way—anger, jealousy, dissatisfaction, irrational requests, criticism—and not allow it to overwhelm her.

You get to be the driver. You may identify many tendencies or inclinations that seem to be inherent traits. Sometimes these characteristics turn out to be symptoms of the underlying drive. Angie's first take on her trait was that she was a bit of a maverick. Then she looked deeper and found that her true trait was a powerful inclination to be fiercely independent; she needed constant verification that "I am not you."

> Traits do not dictate your fate even though they are your gut reactions, your underlying drives.

This more accurate assessment helped her see why she's always the one who is given the long-shot projects because she's not afraid to work without guidelines. But she's also becoming aware this is why her boss rated her as polarizing to the team; she calls it "not needing their permission." They call it not being part of the team.

Angie has amply demonstrated her stand-alone trait by marrying outside her race and culture and, of course, eloping. This trait also means she doesn't like relying on others. Before the year was out, Angie left her large sales firm to start her own business, where fierce independence is a necessary and positive drive. Angie changed her career to honor this drive from the "inner chamber," acknowledging, finally, that this is just the way she is.

Idea Killer

When I was the ace client service agent at JWT, if you had asked about my traits, I would have given you the strengths listed on my résumé: problem solver and strategic thinker. I didn't go any deeper than that.

One of my earlier clues was a reprimand, which I needed, that really slowed me down. In all our creative discussions, I was the first one to jump in to make a summary statement, to give an opinion, to lay out next steps. I relied on my math-solving skills to build logical, irrefutable arguments about why an idea wouldn't work. Bill Ross, then the creative head at JWT, took me aside and hammered me: "You are using your fast read on things and that overly logical brain to stop the flow of ideas in the creative process before they've taken form. You jump in, take over, and kill off good ideas too early."

Idea killer! He might as well have accused me of drowning puppies. He had spotted a clue to a trait of mine, and it was clear I didn't know how to manage it. Being called out forced me to think about the way I was working. I saw I was too impatient to let the messy creative process unfold and I was eager, too eager, to add my thoughts.

I was so intimidated I did not open my mouth in creative reviews for many months. It was the price I paid for not controlling my drive to rush work to a conclusion. Later, I found I was good at seeing the strategic structure in the avalanche of ideas that flow through a creative session, *if* I held back and let others speak and let the ideas morph from a ragged shape into something whole and finished. I was learning to cope with a strong drive. But "Could it be named?" and "Where else would it show up?" I wondered.

There's a helpful way to further distinguish a true trait from those more generic "fear of" ideas or the exterior strengths that emanate from your trait. You can classify that trait as to whether it's positive or negative. It can be both, depending on the situation.

> If it's truly a deep motivation, it will have a negative side and a positive side.

Any trait can be a good cop or a bad cop, depending on how you are provoked to respond in certain situations. If we return to Pauline and Rachel, the clues they spotted seem to be emerging as traits because they do have two sides. Pauline observed that she was always the driver, pushing everything forward, and at work she was the director. "The positive part is that I keep people energized and going forward. I'm just now thinking that it also means I have a 'check the box' mentality and I get bored easily." Pauline locks in on the phrase "What's next?" as how to describe her trait.

Rachel is an anomaly. She hates email or anything that prevents her from seeing things for herself, especially in her business life. "I want to look people in the eye. I think it's because I hate surprises. The negative of that is I overthink, inventing unlikely scenarios and wasting energy on avoiding what never happens. But it's very important to me to find out the truth, the essentials," which is a real positive in her architectural firm and a part of who she is that she likes about herself. Rachel names her trait; she's a "seeker of the truth," in pursuit of a basic integrity of design *and* relationships.

Inspecting your first trait candidates is like turning a coin from side to side to see what each side, the good or the bad, reveals. When such a strong internal force is unleashed, seeing both the positive or negative helps expand your understanding of how your reaction can be disappointment or delight:

Positive		Negative
"I get it done. Always!"	*although*	"I can be domineering."
"I'm dutiful, cooperative."	*but*	"I have no plan of my own."
"I have a strong internal compass."	*still*	"I don't trust anyone."
"I'm inventive, adaptable."	*yet*	"Others suck the energy out of me."

This last observation was from Alice. She called her need to yield to everyone, to give away her energy, "being fluid." She liked her ability to be adaptable, but it had repercussions in connection with her work.

> I like this liquid state. When I was a child, I had several out-of-body experiences. I was at the top of the stairs, but I could see everything going on in the backyard. There's a creative freedom in having no boundaries, but this may be why I sometimes feel more than tired at the end of the workday. I am empty, literally. Can a trait of being both open and fluid or giving it all away be harnessed?

Some of us can name many candidates for traits; too many. We can think of several key qualities that are like tributaries running into the big river of our delivery system. It helps to ignore the smaller streams in order to get to the great currents that form our delivery system. The most helpful test to apply to possible traits is to locate their source.

Where Are These Traits From: Family or Your Own

Screening for the source of your traits is a great device for culling your list. You classify your various interior drives by their most likely provenance. You are asking, "Where does this drive come from?" Focus on the two biggest ones.

To locate the source of the two most dominant traits you've identified, you will find:

- one comes from your family;
- the other is your very own. This is your bred-in-the-bone trait.

Since one big trait will come from the family, we look at family first. The family trait is easier to spot than your own unique trait because it's part of the family lore. You have heard about these tendencies and affinities throughout your childhood. Pause for a moment to consider the first dominant characteristic in your family that comes to mind. For women, the mother is often the source of clues. We women have been studying our mothers for years (not always charitably), and we know who is in there. Often that dominant quality of your mother's has been mirrored in you.

> When you recognize an instinctive family reaction, consider whether or not the rest of the family also has it.

Your family probably has a common trait; it is your family's way of approaching life that you are now using at work. And remember, every trait, even from the family, has a positive and a negative aspect. As Liz explained, "Our family trait is resourcefulness. We can do anything we set our minds to. When I was seven, my father put me on a roof and taught me to shingle it, 'So you'll know, *you'll know*.' It's obviously a good thing at work when the roof is caving in, but the negative is that people tell me I'm too quick to judge their resourcefulness. My answer is, If I can do this, anyone can. Are you really trying?"

Alice, who considered being fluid her own trait, saw a totally different trait when she focused on her family's common trait: "Our way is to always value the group over the individual. My grandparents were coal miners and often unemployed. Anything you had, you were expected to share *with* the group, even a job and its rewards. This is my family's big drive. The negative is that it's left me uneasy about ever speaking up for myself. Since I just got named office head, that group-think has got to go."

When Sam was studying her messages and the influence of her family, their potent statement was: "We (the family) are all we need." Now she takes a look at the family from their trait perspective.

> My family has always revered knowledge and achievement. It's been passed on to each of us from the family gene pool. At first, I couldn't see any negative to that. I mean, how's that a problem? But it does translate to a goal of always striving to be above average. This is true of all my brothers and sisters. It also means there are a lot of people at my office who I feel don't measure up; they're really not above average.

When Sam added, "that includes my boss," we all laughed because that comment follows naturally from her family trait of being quick to rate others. Being superior acting could put quite a damper on a person's career. That's when Sam earned her nickname in the group, Sam of the Clan. The clan members seemed to distance themselves from anyone ordinary, putting Sam alone in her ivory tower. Does that serve her at work?

Can't Wait

My family trait was a virulent form of impatience. This was widely remarked upon by friends and in-laws, usually in the form of criticism: "You people are so fast, always in a hurry."

If you sat at dinner with my family, you might notice that all of us were jiggling our feet under the table. My mother would send me letters, but she'd omit the last page; once I even received an empty envelope. One of our favorite stories, because it had a happy ending, was when Mother left our dog, Phoebe, at the supermarket. Forgotten in the rush but fortunately rescued. This speed at the expense of thoughtfulness and thoroughness was familiar to me, like a fast march tempo.

The positive aspect to this reaction is that I did have a fast take; was quick to pinpoint and assess a problem and come up with a solution. The negative was that I shut others out of the process, losing a lot of useful insight and ideas and leaving people feeling devalued.

Before I became aware of its power, this family trait played havoc with me at work. Over and over, in the collaborative work that is an advertising team, I reached a conclusion before anyone else, without even bothering to include them in my decision process. That was the trait Bill Ross had warned me about all those years ago. This family trait was indeed a crusher of ideas and people. To this day, I recall leaving the room in the dead middle of a presentation by a man I loved and respected. I remember how his face crumpled, and I regret that impatience.

You Have Your Very Own Unique Trait

Though blaming family for all our faults is a great American pastime, we can't lay our second primary trait on them because it is bred in the bone. Like your fingerprint, it belongs only to you. In order to find the powerful drive in us that's not like anyone else's in the family, we have to risk exposing our deepest wishes.

> Your very own trait is the one that will reveal to you the way you want to be at work.

I always wondered what people meant when they said they had "given away their power." Now I get it. This one special way you are at work is your central power source.

This trait tends to show up in a moment of stress, when you say or behave exactly as you feel, in a way that may surprise you as well as others. But you can generally see the results in your trait at work by noticing how people react to you. Like all traits, this essential quality of yours will be both good and bad, and often puzzling as well.

Career Dictator

I honed in on my own bred-in-the-bone trait while I was at Tatham. I knew the label "fearless" my Tatham team had given me was a good quality. But I felt its negative pull, especially when there was no great challenge to face, no overwhelming obstacle to overcome. I would still be out there pushing, maybe overreacting to every incident. Some part of "fearless" could turn into being driven to no purpose, drivenness for its own sake. It exhausted not only me but also my coworkers.

While contemplating this possibly ruthless drive of mine, I remembered an experience in the fifth grade. I was a quiet, skinny little girl, but I was also an aspiring dictator running a group of six girls who followed me, obeyed my rules, accepted my prohibitions, adopted my secret codes.

One day I told a minion to eat my portion of the horrible peas we'd been served at lunch, so I could take my clean plate back for peaches. It was just a minor incident in my well-run kingdom. But a horrified teacher overheard me and marched me into the principal's office. He heard her out, then said, "Leave Charlotte to me."

The principal smiled, patted a chair, and surprised me by handing me a book. "If you're going to run things, you better read this," he said. The title in black block letters was *Leadership*. He was being generous, but all I could hear out of my shame was, "You're trying to take over." It was an uncomfortable thought.

Then another telling episode, nearly as embarrassing, came to mind. I was at a J. Walter Thompson meeting with Sara Lee Foods in our Chicago office. I was the only junior staffer and the only woman. Mark, my supervisor, had invited me to observe. I'm sure he expected me to be seen and not heard. Well, I spoke up anyway. After all, I was probably the only one in the room who knew how to cook, and I had previously worked at a food company. Why wouldn't they want to hear my ideas for new bakery products? I didn't even see the dirty looks a sniggering coworker told me about later. "Mark wanted to kill you when you were blurting away."

When we met for a debriefing a week later, Mark opened with, "Sara Lee wants to meet with us again, but they don't want you to come," turning to me. "You talk too much." Then he let out a big laugh. There it was again. I wanted to speak out and I wanted to run things even when I had little to offer and didn't know what I was talking about.

At Tatham, when I had to undergo an intense self-scrutiny to find out if I could even handle this new job, it finally came to me: the trait that was my deep interior way of working. It wasn't that I was a fearless leader or an ill-advised dictator. It was that . . . ALL THINGS BEING EQUAL, I'D RATHER BE IN CHARGE.

This was my own trait, quite separate from the family trait of flaming impatience. It's not as delicious a trait as fearlessness, but it's equally problematic for a woman in a man's world. I felt in my bones that this was my true nature. I could now match many of my experiences, mistakes, and victories to this intrinsic drive, this instinctive reaction I had to the various challenges I'd faced.

A drive to be in charge when you're not qualified or welcome is an invitation to fail early and publicly; that's the negative. A desire to take charge when there's heart-stopping trouble and you still like the idea of jumping in is well suited to the challenge of turning a broken company around.

These powerful drives will be heard from, ready or not.

These two interior driving priorities of mine, fast to act and an in-charge inclination, dictated what would turn out to be my life's work. Because of these traits, I would become known as a turnaround specialist, an agent of change. There's great freedom in being clear about the part of you that you can't change anyway. It frees you to openly reveal your instinctive reactions to others, and it helps you to guide your own actions, even helps you to set up a few roadblocks occasionally so you don't run amok. Anything running that strongly within needs watching, appreciating, and handling. If you're not aware of it, it can get the better of you. And even when you are conscious of it, it often needs to be modified to suit the situation.

THE CHAMELEON

When Rachel was considering the source of her traits, she decided the "truth seeker" trait was passed along from her mother and her stepfather. With them, it was more a case of being careful, to dig in and reveal all aspects of something before they made a move. In her work, when a client asks too many questions or becomes demanding, Rachel has to arrange for a personal meeting before she is comfortable that she knows what's going on. That's how she expresses the family inherited trait at work.

Now, challenged to find the trait that's her very own, Rachel's face lights up and, unlike others in the group, she can name this quality of hers immediately: "I am a chameleon. I can fit in anywhere. I can juggle many points of view. When a project is off the rails, like a new city building, I will eventually bring everyone together; the city zoning group, the builder, the politician, the disturbed neighborhood."

When pressed to find the negative, since this all seemed so positive, she reluctantly added, "I rate empathy above all. But I'm in trouble if there's anger or heavy hostility; then I completely withdraw."

Your trait may be what drives you, but that does not necessarily mean everyone else will make room for your particular interior will to drive; they are concerned with expressing their own traits.

Your Drive Way

C. S. Lewis, whom you may know for his work *The Chronicles of Narnia*, the children's story of magic and goodness, is also a philosopher I pay attention to. He asks some good questions. One is, "What kind of machine were you given to drive?" He discusses, for example, if one is given a perfect machine, such as a good heart, a generous nature, great beauty, or other such idealized attributes, then the driving is pretty easy. But most of us have to accept some compromises and create our own opportunities as we make our way to the workplace with the machine we were given.

These two traits—the big one from the family gene pool and your own rare energy source—determine a great deal about how you drive. There are more influences to factor in as well to get the whole picture, but laying out these two prevailing drives will at least describe the boundaries of your drive way.

When taken together, do these abiding qualities of yours magnify who you are at work? Does one have priority over the other? The importance of being a neutral investigator of your deeper drives comes down to balancing the weight of these traits:

> You can hold these drives of yours in check; you can give one more breathing room than the other.

In your investigation, you have accepted the good, the bad, even the ugly of strong inward motivations, but that does not mean they are allowed to career through the workday unguided by you. You're the driver.

The combination of my drives operating without any awareness on my part sent me to the new job at Tatham completely defenseless. That polite word I attached to my universal family quality of impatience translated to a cocky impetuousness at leaving J. Walter Thompson to join a new company. I never took the time, or expended the energy, to dig into Tatham and see what I was moving toward. I was full of a superficial and brittle (as in breakable) self-confidence. But this trait of impatience could turn into a dangerous level of thoughtlessness; it was the equivalent of driving blind. This inherent quality married to my other trait, a great thirst to run things, explains why I hit a wall. That wall tempted me to take the other "safe" agency job offered me just months before I was to be CEO. Had I done that, I could have avoided ever naming my traits and would not have taken the measure of myself, carrying yet another external message—that I left because I couldn't cut it.

I have not truly conquered my tendency to move too fast. But I am always watching for it and pulling back. In a recent Martha Stewart board meeting, Frederic Fekkai, another member and close friend, nudged me when I was about to run right over an important comment. But at the end of that meeting, there was an opportunity for me to make a contribution. If you want to verify that your set of traits is spot-on, see if they resonate with someone you trust, who works with you. I guarantee you they will say (at least to one of them), "Of course that's how you are."

MARTHA'S FAMILY TRAIT

I could make a pretty good guess as to Martha Stewart's other trait, the one from her family. Her mother and father were both teachers. This is expressed in Martha as a powerful desire to share what she knows. She cannot bear to leave us in the dark. This, in concert with a great intellectual curiosity, has earned her a very large stage, and these two traits are her guiding principles whether she's helping design houses, studying how dogs sleep, or teaching what makes a good soil.

In case you're wondering, Martha's dominant traits have a good side and a bad side too. When Martha is learning something, she's an irresistible force. Once I watched while a tall, handsome fellow who owned a tree farm was explaining the care of certain trees to Martha. He was clearly captivated by her careful attention and slight smile, and the way she leaned forward to hear his every word. When she finally turned away, I thought he might fall over, released so suddenly from that intensity of hers. She has a degree of focus on learning I've never seen in anyone else. But at dinner, when the conversation is casual, the group just chatting, the food already assessed, she can fall dead asleep; she's bored, gone. I stay in kicking range in case she needs a wake-up call.

Balancing the Traits

As the women in the workshops have a full first look at both of their big driving traits, they begin to judge them in tandem, evaluating how the combination affects their work.

Too Close

Rachel felt her inherited trait of doing anything to avoid surprises, to exercise caution, worked too closely with her own peacemaker trait that she respected and wanted to enhance.

> Yes, I am a chameleon. I fit in everywhere. I can hear many points of view and will bring different viewpoints together.
>
> But when you add to that the tendency to dodge unpredictability (as our family put it), I feel like I become too much the great mediator, a role I always took at home too. Mediators can be compromisers as an excuse to avoid a big fight. These two traits seem to double up the impact of one another.

In Sync

Surprisingly, Gwen's traits worked together to make her job a perfect fit for her. Her family trait inspired in their children a wide-ranging interest in how things work:

> We read Proust at the dining table and the *Farmer's Almanac*. But my own personal drive is a quality that can almost be a curse. I am acutely sensitive to every nuance and each person around. I know what they're thinking and what they want. At times, I am overwhelmed. I hear and sense too much.

For a world-class public relations firm in Washington, D.C., Gwen's traits are an asset. There's a different business every week to master, which fits in with Gwen's trait of having a wide array of interests. Almost everyone who comes to the firm is in trouble or is facing a quandary of some kind. Gwen's incredible ability to sense such complex tangles, often never spoken aloud, amazes her cohorts. "She's a witch. She knows it before they even tell us."

Double Impact

Carolyn's two traits complemented her so well they put her on the most valuable player list at her engineering firm. Her family passed along to her that work was the solution to everything. They did not believe in stinting or bargaining; work was deadly serious and a large part of the point of life. Carolyn's summary: "Well, it's an awesome work ethic." She's the one who said, "I never quit." Now she knows this to be a direct family mandate.

She didn't take long to name her own bred-in-the-bone nature either. She said, "*I will stand*; there's a fire burning in me. I am willing to challenge, to stretch myself. In college, I asked the professor for a review of my A-minus, I deserved an A."

When she put these two traits together, Carolyn also learned why she felt she had trouble "scaling myself. I can't modulate very well. It's all here in my traits. These are the great directors that explain my ambition and why my boss told me to take a chill pill."

If that inner fire is banked, smothered under what people expect of you, who they *think* you are, or by your own lack of awareness, you will stray far from your highest potential.

Now that you have an introduction to your own fired-up inner inclinations, these traits are yours; to know, to honor . . . and to manage.

> There is a fire burning in all of us that can propel us forward to speak out or to stand up when needed.

4

SELF-PORTRAIT
Who You Think You Are

WHEN YOU TRULY know who you are, you can harness all the parts of you that contribute to your life at work to activate your full potential. This larger self-image will keep you steady and upright in the face of obstacles. Without it, in the words of the poet Rainer Maria Rilke, you could find yourself "standing on fishes."

I saw this happen to a good man who had no idea how to find the center from which he could stand. George, a much respected client of Tatham's, was a senior officer at Nabisco. He was a rugged Santa type— white hair, easy manner, rolling laugh—and he was a pro, a veteran marketer of Nabisco's well-loved brands. But when he was caught up by a new management group, he could not stand steady; he was left slipping and sliding about. George was afflicted by a toxic form of accommodation: "Tell me who you want me to be."

Nabisco was acquired in a takeover by a swashbuckling, hard-edged crew from the world of high finance. They brought a raw, rough culture that included swearing, late-night drinking bouts, celebrity parties. It was as if a band of pirates had boarded the good ship Nabisco. They viewed brands as chess pieces, even requiring their officers to change positions often so they wouldn't get too "attached" to a particular position or brand. Everyone had to keep moving, unsteady and ever anxious about what to expect next.

George took on a new style that included heavy drinking, a sharper, shinier wardrobe, and an irritable demeanor, which caused him to raise his voice frequently. He even started smoking again. Where had our Santa gone? Our sturdy, steady marketing pro?

One week our team was in San Francisco with George when the account manager called, nearly shouting into the phone, "Sarah just quit." My heart tumbled. Sarah was a pivotal player in this delicate stage of our agency turnaround, the face of the new Tatham. Before I could even ask, he went on, "George called her a cunt! Sarah said it was like watching a snake come out of his mouth."

Agencies are no strangers to edgy language, but I realized I had never once heard this word spoken aloud. Clearly I had to confront George. I plunged in during the first minutes of our meeting, "George, would you call your daughter a cunt?" I asked. His head jerked back as though he'd been hit. "Well, Sarah is like my daughter and you cannot speak to her or, in fact, to any of us, that way."

His shoulders sagged and he looked gray; in fact he looked ill. Not long after our meeting, he checked into his hometown hospital with a bleeding ulcer. His body couldn't handle the betrayal. Had George known what a good guy he was, he could have held on to his own truer way of working. Rejecting the role of pirate, he could have coped with the new regime and not been left "standing on fishes." Pirates are never in for the long haul; they grab the treasure and leave. All but one of the takeover crew was gone in eighteen months. Sarah, I'm happy to report, stayed at Tatham. George went into the restaurant business with his cousin; this time the fish were on the table.

———— ✄ ————

There are many ways to lose your sense of who you are at work: a new position, a public failure, any challenge that leaves you unnerved. What George lacked was a steady and strongly defined self-image.

Consolidation: All of You

Now that you have made your excavation and have become better acquainted with the messages you have taken in and have identified your inner drivers, it's time to pull it all together into a fully formed image of yourself. Portrait making is an act of integration.

You are integrating:

External qualities: Your familiar job strengths and weaknesses
Your education and skills
Internal messages: Family Influences
Traits: Internal drivers
Insights

All of these factors, the traits, the messages, the qualities listed on your résumé, plus your fresh assessment of them, can now be melded together in a self-portrait. Believe it or not, it will all come together in a compelling vision that not only guides you day to day but gives you a picture of who you can become.

The women whose stories you followed in earlier chapters are your "partners" once again, for they can show you how they knitted all these pieces together to form their own self-portraits.

Alice

Alice is our first portrait maker. Alice's family message was that it's important to always put on a good show. Alice believes this tendency has won her a positive office reputation for being a skillful diplomat. Her family also emphasized the value of the group over the individual: one for all and all for one. That was also an influential message, as you'll see.

However, Alice's own trait became the most dominant feature in her portrait: she is fluid, flexible, and inventive. As she weighed the positive and negative aspects of this trait, Alice discovered a darker side of being fluid and flexible: she is boundary free.

Although she now heads the office in Detroit, she realizes she has no boundaries when it comes to supervising her team; she covers for them, does endless counseling, feels constantly pulled to address everyone else's needs.

Putting her features in order of their importance to her, she created this list:

Trait: I'm inventive and flexible, but I'm also sucked dry daily.
Message: The group matters more than any individual.
Message: Keep that mask on.
Résumé: Diplomatic (accommodating) Alice.

Alice is presenting the harshest view of who she is. It's a diagnostic tool for her; she wants to focus on how the qualities interact with each other and influence her delivery system. Alice's first portrait managed to convey the whole web of relationships at her office, including how she sees her own role at the center of things. These words are a powerful image for the complex nature of how and why Alice works the way she does:

BEFORE SELF-PORTRAIT

I see myself as a
FLOODING PLAIN.
"Everyone is irrigating off my waters."

While devastatingly clear, this is no blueprint for the future. Alice's assessment of what she learned about herself inspired this rather ruthless look at herself.

I have found the smallest possible way to use my significant ability to find inventive solutions and get everyone to sign on. *I don't use it to lead.* I just use it to make a happy team. This fluid nature means I'm the irrigator, and also the Queen of Compromises, making sure the group's happy, my stage mask firmly in place.

The women found there needs to be a way to express the insights they've gained, a picture of the messages and the consequences of their powerful interior drivers. These implications can't be ignored; shedding or enhancing or rerouting may be called for. That's why they constructed a "before" portrait.

> The women taught me that there has to be a "before" portrait.

By interpreting what you've learned, ranked in order of importance to you, you are creating a before portrait. This step allows you to see where you are, before you think about what your more forward-looking self-image should be.

Alice says, "I'm still drawing on what I've learned, but I want to rescue qualities of mine that have gotten lost; I *am* decisive, I *can* nail a problem down; it's no small thing that I can invent new solutions. *I'm* still fluid, but I'm preparing to shed that 'group' idea. I want to appreciate the power that comes from being self-directed, not group-directed. Here are the ways I want to actually lead this office."

After Self-Portrait

I'm a MIGHTY RIVER BOUND BY MOUNTAINS AND FORESTS.
"No one tells this river where to go."

The river has replaced the seeping plain, but Alice believes her fluid nature is central to who she is. "Whether I am whitewater rapids or a still calm, I am the one directing the current, but I need those boundaries, that shore."

Your portrait is a private set of codes. Alice's new portrait activates a picture in her mind of how she is going to earn that seat at the table as the new office head. But even as outsiders, we can see a huge difference

> The after portrait is a sum of what you've learned about yourself plus your surface self, making it larger, fuller.

between depicting yourself as a "flooding plain" or as the "mighty Colorado River."

Behavior at work can become so automatic, so "ordained" by old habits and outdated views that you can fail to realize you've lost yourself, as George did and as Alice is investigating. She had ceased to be fluid and inventive in order to become an irrigating system for everyone else. Alice, in the going-forward vision she calls her after self-portrait, does not abandon herself; she defines how she will activate the power within her. She's learned that her ability to be fluid, moving, free-flowing is a creative quality of her very own.

How Portraits Are Formed

The before portrait acknowledges dominant qualities that may need to be modified or evaluated. The after portrait is your guide, a picture of who you intend to be.

- You ask, What's wrong with this picture? In order to build the before portrait, you accept that any one of your aspects may be far stronger than the others.
- You use your after portrait to set new priorities, to honor your heartfelt desires, and to act as your compass.
- The point of this portrait, your fuller self-image, is to connect all of who you are with the way you work.

There is a heightened level of self-awareness that feels fresh and raw. I think that's why the women in the workshops have wanted to deal with what's wrong first in the before portrait. Women can be impressively direct and honest in their assessments.

We may go to work initially to hide behind our well-performing selves, but once we look at the inner chamber and review the messages, the dawning realizations and new understandings quickly re-place the resistance of "I won't go there." Women are now free to ask, "What is *wrong* or right with this picture?"

Carolyn

Carolyn is an engineer with a firm in Dallas. She was raised on the Boston shore, and that environment affected how she constructed her picture of herself. Carolyn created a before portrait as critical as Alice's. When she began to integrate the messages, focusing on one dominant trait aided by her office reputation, she felt backed into a corner or, as she put it, "swimming on the bottom."

> External: I am, by far, the hardest worker and everyone knows it.
> Message: Remember, men will be chosen first.
> Family trait: Work is the whole point of life.
> Insight: I can never quit. I work through every illness. I'm afraid I might not give true value.

Carolyn's boss told her to "take a chill pill" when she was named the youngest vice president in her engineering firm. The odd thing is, Carolyn's traits seemed admirable. They made her a favorite in her company. She was intensely hardworking (a family trait), and she had a fire inside to encourage standing up at work, never quitting (her own trait). But Carolyn sees a consequence here that the rest of us would miss:

> That hard work trait of the family has called all the shots. I haven't really stood up for myself in a long time. If you put all this together, it's like our old family saying, "Climb the mountain; don't use oxygen." I have things out of proportion. That's why this is my before self-portrait: I'm an OCTOPUS.
> I hold on to too much. I'm stuck at the bottom, watching everyone above me swimming freely.

The octopus, moving through the depths, tentacles reaching everywhere for duties, is the picture of what's wrong to Carolyn, what she wants to change. If she had accepted the congratulations from her company at face value on how hard she worked, she'd still be a bottom feeder. "The men all have time to laugh and joke, to take on interesting projects."

Carolyn has found another water creature to symbolize how she wants to behave and be seen at work going forward:

AFTER SELF-PORTRAIT

I'm
A DOLPHIN.
"I know when to come up for air."
"It's my time to be a dolphin. Graceful, relaxed, I know
I am deserving of attention, but on my terms.
People come to see me perform . . . and they pay well for it."

A dolphin has all kinds of engaging qualities that the sand crawling octopus does not have. "No one thinks of the dolphin as a slacker. Dolphins delight us with their wit and playfulness. It's not against the work police to be engaging as well as hardworking and confident."

That dolphin carries a lot of implications for Carolyn's directive to herself. At the moment, she feels underpaid and somewhat sidelined; the dolphin would not stand for that. After traveling through the messages, the traits, and her office behavior, she realized that in fact she is more than earning her way. "I worked to the limit to prove I was valuable; that's the octopus. The dolphin is my picture of learning to carry confidence in myself to work."

My Portrait, My Compass

After I learned to understand my personal behavior at Tatham, the way that I always seemed to want to run things and fast (my traits), I needed a fuller picture of myself at work. I wanted to embrace my love of work, but I needed to control those unruly drives of mine. My own message suitcase was full of fears that I would be smothered by debt, inadequate to lead, and impotent at dealing with the drink and drug culture. I knew I could be fearless defending the good people. I was able to stave off their anxiety when I was a back-against-the-wall kid, even as I faced my own fears at 4:00 AM every morning.

Part of my portrait was an inspiration I found in George Bernard Shaw's words; they were like a clarion call to me to use all my talent on behalf of good work. They articulated my desire to test my largest self at work. Shaw and I believe:

> This is the true joy in life, the being used for a purpose recognized by yourself as a mighty one; the being thoroughly worn out before you are thrown on the scrap heap; the being a force of Nature instead of a feverish selfish little clod of ailment and grievances complaining that the world will not devote itself to making you happy.

Shaw's words evoke the fear I had when I almost gave up on myself at Tatham in my darkest hour: "to be a feverish, selfish little clod of ailment and grievances." I leaned instead on his image for standing tall, to be a "force of nature."

I knew I was only halfway to my portrait because it didn't address exactly how I intended to be something as fierce as a force of nature. As an unharnessed force, I could be rude and ruthless. I discovered a young woman who came to embody my best self. She was more symbolic than real. I endowed her with gifts I wished to emulate and carried her in my mind's eye as a companion to Shaw's bold words.

I'd seen her on a family vacation to the Tennessee mountains when I was thirteen years old. Walking alone on a path, I sensed a presence. I looked up to see a young woman sitting very still on a beautiful roan horse. She looked down at me intently from her post atop the hill. Some kind of recognition passed between us. On her wrists, I saw beautiful bracelets of deep reddish gold, sparkling in the light. As though I'd known her always, I asked, "What are they?" She knew exactly what I meant. "My father gave them to me, for strength."

To me, she was perfect. Astride her horse at her post on a hill, she had her weapons and her careful courtesy. I thought, "This is who I will become." I never saw her again, but I have never lost the sense of her.

> The act of creating a self-portrait takes all of you into the tent.

We spend way too many hours at work not to aim for the fullest, most enriching experience. Our portrait is a compass. You can see how these three examples—the mighty river, the dolphin, my woman on a hill—set up a picture of our future intentions: to move as a powerful current, to be joyful at work, to achieve a mighty purpose. We are guided by these, our best self pictures.

Portraits Express What You Want for Yourself

Implicit in the words, pictures, mottos, or symbols you choose to represent yourself is a promise of what you intend for yourself.

When else do you really stop and think about such things? We can be asked sterile questions such as, Where do you want to be in five years? And the mandatory answer (taught in graduate school) to that question is, "CEO" or, "in your job." Not much of an answer. There's only room for one person in those slots, and it indicates that you think "up" is the only goal.

Since women often refrain from taking their own career as firmly in hand as men do, your portrait becomes a reminder, an aid to help you do just that. Before you know it, you will be making vows to yourself, as Rachel did.

Rachel

Rachel was dealing with a great mix of discoveries, all of which seemed equally important at first: "I see that I learned to be a mediator, in part because my family hates surprises, and we had plenty of those. That's why I must see people eye to eye. That did help me become a gifted collaborator, and people think I have great personal chemistry."

She now wonders why all this doesn't feel so successful.

I was the family mediator between a succession of stepfathers and Mom. That means I've spent a lot of my personal and professional life accommodating others. No wonder I take on the fixer side of being a manager.

And I must seem frail, as my boss says no one wants to hurt my feelings. People try to protect me from anything ugly because I urge peace, I guess. Somehow this "protection" translates to no salary increases in a long time and a heavier workload and my boss taking all the credit. This is my before picture; it's not pretty.

BEFORE SELF-PORTRAIT

I'm LITTLE RED RIDING HOOD
running into the forest, staving off the world,
making sure Grandma is okay, even defanging
the wolf (big client), tra la, la la through the woods.

This is who I vow to be no longer. I don't want to be protected by others as in a fairy tale (or to be eaten either). The question is, do I have to completely reinvent myself?

Rachel returned to her source of pride in an interior strength, found in both her traits:

We are a family who seeks the truth. I'm nourished by that and it does send me to look 'em in the eye. But my own trait as a chameleon (you can drop me anywhere and I'll fit in) has to be a good thing in a world changing so fast. I need to focus on new goals to honor these traits.

I don't want to use all these talents just to keep the peace; at least the kind of peace that's esteem robbing and self-sacrificing.

AFTER SELF-PORTRAIT

"I want to make constructive change."

Rachel's new promise to herself is "I am on a truth mission, in pursuit of big, important changes in design and in relationships. It's more about conflict resolution than, 'Let's all be friends.'"

Here are her new terms for engagement, her new priorities: "I don't want to be protected, the peacemaker. I want to be responsible, to bring about important change."

Rachel's bulletin board is an extension of her portrait. She collected stories of people who brought change to others and even to countries by first resolving conflicts in order to make important contributions. Rachel didn't throw out her talents of mediating or her charming, charismatic way of working. She just redirected them toward a larger goal.

> What you've learned about yourself can encourage you to focus on what you want out of work.

Considering what they want rather than what the company or others want is for many women their first bold act of self-determination. We wouldn't dream of treating our company products or projects in a rudderless fashion. We can be as boundary free as Alice if we don't have a guide to depict our own vision.

In Gwen's case, it wasn't a matter of boundaries. The portrait exercise was a matter of learning to lead or losing her moment to lead.

Gwen

Gwen was our poster child for a woman beset by mixed messages; her first portrait was really ambivalence. Gwen knows she needs a more supportive portrait than ambivalence, but her choices are more complex than most. Given her own trait of acute sensitivity to every discussion, opinion, and reaction (stated or not), she walks in a daily minefield of her own reactions. Among the inconsistent messages from home, there was one that mattered more when she was named a top manager: "Throttle back. Don't be too successful or people will hate you."

Hiding behind "I don't believe in empty self-promotion," Gwen was taking no credit for her brilliant ideas, allowing other team members to bask in her deflected glory. No wonder she was ambivalent. Gwen felt like an actress in someone else's play. Now her challenges lay in taking on the leadership role, out there in the spotlight, risking all that envy. She wanted to claim her true self, her love of striving, her interest in a range of subjects, and above all, her successes.

As she was rewriting how she would be a leader, a blow knocked her off her path. She was listed among the top women leaders in her field of public relations and was scheduled to be interviewed in a big press article. She swallowed hard and steeled herself to handle it personally rather than pushing the credits and the interviews off on someone else. Her New York corporate office decided to put out a congratulatory ad. It was every bit as nasty as Gwen feared. She is shown in a circus ring, snapping her whip at men seated on stools. That ad created laughter, maybe a little admiration, certainly a lot of jealousy.

Gwen has spent enough time doing her excavation to understand there are these kind of consequences to stepping into the spotlight. She made a decision to fight rather than fold. Very out of character (for her), she printed up her own ad, sent it to friends, and pinned it up on the display board in her office. Her headline, a quote she liked: "You say I'm a bitch, like that's a bad thing." And her resolve: "I am an ambitious woman out in front. I will not diminish myself because your definition of ambition in a woman is bitchiness."

After that challenging episode, Gwen realized she had voiced her future portrait; it is leading, but on her terms:

AFTER SELF-PORTRAIT

"I am a CONDUCTOR.
I conduct from the center of who I am."

She wants to be clear that there are amazing musicians and a splendid score at this concert, but she *will* take the conductor's baton.

Portraits Have Heart

Any portrait you create needs to include your heart, not just your brain, and your will. In accomplishing day-to-day tasks, you may leave your beliefs, your feelings, what matters most to you, on the side as you do the work, but your portrait has to include those things because it conveys all the vital aspects of who you are as you engage with others.

That mysterious young woman who stood for my best self was like a still life stamped in my mind's eye. Her strength, her preparation, her bracelets, her resolve all meant something to me. I read into that young woman on the hill everything I would need for those times when I was low and ill equipped and when words alone, not even Shaw's, would suffice.

David Whyte, who is called the poet of the workplace, tells of being reminded of the role of the heart at work. Even though he really believed in the not-for-profit company he worked for, he found his days terribly tiring, often frustrating. At the end of yet another long day, he met up with a close friend who was a Buddhist monk. Seeing his hanging head and his body limp with fatigue, the monk said, "The cure for exhaustion is not rest; it is wholeheartedness."

> Learning to act on your instincts, your deeper passions, and your most valued beliefs will give you greater power at work.

In constructing the portrait, we need to draw on these experiences when our heart felt most whole, most alive; or the opposite of that, dead. If you do nothing more than use your portrait to display and stay in touch with your innermost feelings and desires, to check in on how your heart is responding, you will be honoring yourself.

The power to influence that comes from expressing wholehearted parts of yourself is demonstrated by the great lengths to which the U.S. State Department goes to scrub all such emotion, passion, and shades of meaning out of every foreign affairs missive. The idea is to convey information with *no* extra meaning. It's called scrubbing.

I came across the act of scrubbing, stripping away any heart from government-to-government messages in order to reduce them to the facts. They were to be totally devoid of imagination or ideas that would inspire or influence, so that no one could make a loose interpretation of what the United States meant to say. It could be a statement from Secretary Powell, a wording in a treaty, a cable between the U.S. foreign office and China. It was scrubbed to death, stripped of any evocative word, cleaned of any possible hint of feelings or opinion. Traveling, as such messages must, through a web of lies, at least fifty foreign languages, biases, and opposing customs, it had to be bare (boring) bones. These messages had only one mission: to inform.

But in your messages to the work world, you can choose to inspire, relate, influence, *and* inform. In fact, it's vital that you do so.

Your portrait can help keep you from being scrubbed clean, leaving your heart unused and inert. It's exhausting to be someone less than yourself. That's working with half a heart, and it's the source of the wiped out, lonely, and discouraged feelings that so many working women experience.

Lydia

Lydia was "scrubbed" as clean as a government missive. Opening up emotionally in any way was tough for her. As Lydia traveled through her family messages and made an inventory of her traits, she concluded that the problem was a compounding of messages and traits.

"Stay out of the drama" was the word from her mother. Another expression of this family trait was an intense level of independence, passed along by her father, as "never let them see you sweat." Lydia also sees how those in the office react to her scrubbing as well.

I know I'm seen as unapproachable, but I feel I can't "emote" at all, ever. My boss called me "Ms. Teflon," but admiringly, when we had to fire some people. I showed no emotion, of course. That's how I came to this before portrait.

Before Self-Portrait

"I'm a beautiful carved ICE SCULPTURE on a banquet table. I have a dangerous, time-sensitive portrait; I'm melting away."

The trouble is, this picture doesn't do justice to my own valuable trait of being able to intensely focus when we need solutions. I can solve any sales problem, but as the ice lady, no one will think of me. I only have one choice: I have to find a way to be more approachable.

Lydia kept returning to memories of when her heart was engaged, before she closed it off. "It was at family storytelling time (before I outgrew them). That is where I found a portrait that is like a constant inspiration to me."

After Self-Portrait

LET ME TELL YOU MY STORY.
"I will open up, let others in, and be vulnerable."
("I say this with my arms wide open,
exposing my heart; well, figuratively, anyway.")

She knew you can't just *say* your heart's in it; you have to *show* it. She picked a test assignment, crawling her way cautiously forward:

I went to my boss, nervous and shaky. After all, he had called me Ms. Teflon. But he is a loyal supporter, so I was able to be honest. I told him that, in fact, I didn't handle firing those people well at all. "It tore me up" were my exact words. Honestly, his mouth was hanging open. I think he was a little disappointed to lose his one objective, female soldier, but it costs me too much.

This ongoing presentation of who I am at the office means I'll have to trust that I can show I care a lot, that I sweat, that, in fact, sometimes I'm on fire.

Just promoted as the only woman among four men running the sales department of a huge health care organization, she said, "They shy away from me. They have their own club. Entering this big boys' club, that's next."

Lydia has now set much bigger expectations for herself: openness to vulnerability and a willingness to be exposed. That's having your heart in your work.

Portraits Go into Battle with You

In her book *What's Holding You Back?* Linda Austin explains that when women can't fully grasp the nature of who they want to be at work, they end up settling for less. They promise themselves, "I'll be good, but not great," which Linda memorably calls "slipping out of a side exit." Part of how you communicate what you think of yourself is your wardrobe, your hair, how you see yourself.

Kirsten

Kirsten's appearance was a daily visual of settling for less. A woman of thirty-four, she looked twenty-two. Her clothes were interesting but messy, as were her curls and wandering bangs. I was surprised to read that Kirsten was a supervisor of a creative department whose company handled sales events and sales promotions. In spite of her success at nailing down great results on once lost causes, she'd been assigned the thankless no-name products like toothbrushes and mud flaps for trucks. She felt plateaued and taken for granted.

Kirsten had one of the most explosive journeys through the excavation; in her home there was not a single functioning adult, though it included a large and changing cast of characters. As the oldest of four children, Kirsten was the gatekeeper between the other kids and chaos.

Her first portrait caught, painfully, how she had transferred this coping system to her work:

BEFORE SELF-PORTRAIT

"I am a SCARECROW
blown here and there
by every wind, always defending,
keeping away the invaders."

This empty figure is not really who Kirsten is, but she's reflecting a style created by a dangerous childhood where as the eldest, she literally "saved the crop" over and over again. The scarecrow image depressed her, but it also put her on alert.

That's not my job anymore—to fend off. Also I have to remember that scarecrows are only stuffed with straw, dressed in old rags. (I do dress down, wearing casual girly stuff at the office. I saw it as a vote for the creative spirit.) I know I'm not a hollowed-out empty husk, but I have to work out who is really in there.

Her family memories, and the role she took as gatekeeper, far outweighed her ability to see her own qualities. She wrote out a twelve-page answer to the five questions about her family messages. It was a childhood saga from hell. A druggie mother, three abusive stepfathers, and only Kirsten to protect her younger brothers and sister. She managed to keep her eyes on the prize, "Kirsten at Work." When she got to gifts, she came up with clue to her interior strength. "I've been through a lot. I'm a lot tougher than I look."

Kirsten's own trait, which emerged from this bundle of troubles, is that she has an untiring source of energy, a really stunning capacity to keep on keepin' on. So far, it had left her doing all the thankless small jobs and supervising a team of disenchanted writers. But she drew a new picture: it was a steel rod.

I am strong inside, like steel, but it doesn't show. I see that the disastrous family life we had as children has made me stronger than most. I've lived through several lifetimes; work is pure pleasure compared to my early home life

After Self-Portrait

I have a SPINE OF STEEL.

I'm not a defenseless little girl anymore. I need to erase that image. I am ready to stop getting blown around by every wind. When I sat with my own bred-in-the-bone trait of untiring resilience, I quit giving up on myself.

Kirsten has a new resolve to take on her rather indifferent boss. Now she has a compass—a woman supported by a steel rod running through her spine.

Kirsten and I were to meet in New York. I wanted to see what a steel rod does for the posture and the self-esteem. To tell you the truth, I wouldn't have recognized her. I watched this executive woman walk confidently toward me, her heels clicking in the hall, and it was Kirsten. She noted my amazement and enjoyed it. Blond hair sleeked back, a mismatched top to bottom suit, but the kind we all want to copy, carrying a beautiful pink leather portfolio case. Since I was still mute with amazement, she volunteered, "It's going to be easier for me. I've decided to grow up. There'll be a grown-up woman in that portrait."

> From straw to steel. It's an arresting comparison. It captures the imagination. Think what it does for Kirsten.

My Portrait Goes into Battle

At Tatham, I was feeling smug. We had some success and I was feeling assured that I was the right manager to transform our agency; my portrait was leaning more toward "she's a force of nature" than the quiet, strong woman on her mount. But she was the one I needed in a battle I soon faced.

I was six years into my career at Tatham as the now highly lauded CEO, known in the Chicago ad world and beyond for successfully pitting our medium-size agency against the sprawling worldwide giants. I was proud, almost arrogant about what we'd done.

Our newest client, the marketer of several big name beer brands, included high-powered guys who were not accustomed to women managers, so I stuck to my gender-neutral persona of being smart and professional. Even so, it turns out a test was in the offing.

Out of the blue, Howard, their big group vice president, invited me to dinner in New York to discuss our agency-client relationship, a surprising invitation given his level. But I was happy to take my briefcase and high expectations to the "mountain," the top guy. When I walked into the 21 Club, Howard and his cronies turned to size me up in a very overt way. I instantly felt very uncomfortable. I gathered that these fellows had been at the bar for awhile.

Howard casually suggested that I get rid of my car and driver so we could ride in his limo to the restaurant. I felt a trickle of anxiety. I went over to my driver, but not to tell him to leave. Even as a young girl, I always liked to have an exit plan. "Please follow us," I told him. God bless New York limo drivers because he whispered back, "Never fear. I'll stay with you."

As we settled into Howard's car, he suddenly slapped the seat. "I forgot the papers we'll need. Driver, stop at the Helmsley Hotel first." Then he turned to me, "You know, you should come up with me and see our new company apartment. It's pretty smashing." I knew how much my partners would love to hear about this inner sanctum in the sky, so I readily agreed.

I was startled that the company had its own private elevator. In that small space, the smell of booze coming from Howard was overwhelming; he seemed unsteady. I began to feel my all-powerful CEO shield drain away as I realized I might be in serious trouble.

The elevator opened directly onto the hushed company suite. This was not good. No one would believe I'd come innocently to his private hotel room. Howard grabbed me abruptly and muttered, "Let me show you around." He pushed me into a dark room and I fell right over onto the bed without even seeing it. Suddenly he was right there beside me, encircling me. He was startlingly strong, oblivious to my struggle to escape. I started to panic—how could it be that less than an hour after meeting this man, I was fighting him off on a bed in a dark hotel room?

I became a terrified, overwhelmed woman. My throat locked up so I could not make a sound. I felt completely helpless. I gave up. Then a gust of pure anger blew through me. I thought about my long journey to rescue our agency, how we had all fought every step of the way. Was I going to lose that by being tossed around by this Neanderthal? Then my woman on the horse appeared, calming, steadying me. I began a silent defense. "I am not your victim, Howard. You don't know me. I am strong in a way you will never be . . . a force of nature."

I found I could speak out loud: "Howard, you don't want to do this." At that, I gave him a mighty shove. To my surprise, he rolled over easily, like a ball, and came to sit on the opposite edge of the bed. As I raced to the door, praying I could find the elevator button, I heard sobs, great heaving sobs behind me.

Trembling head to toe, I descended to the lobby, the beautiful, busy lobby. Easing myself into the car, I realized all I had to call on was an untapped inner strength, that was enough.

What had Howard been thinking? I suspect he'd imagined that something romantic could happen if we met in New York. In his drunken state, he must have seen himself as a conqueror, showing the new woman how masterful, how irresistible he was. That was his portrait.

I tell this story not to warn against private elevators, but to assure you that this is really how self-image can do battle for you. I felt untouchable as CEO, but that was my exterior, somewhat overconfident self. When that was shattered, I had to rely on a deeper reality. I was able to see myself as a woman who was armed; bracelets, resolve, integrity.

> We are women, we will be tested. And in those tests, you need to know what you have inside that you can call on.

I hope you'll never need to call on your portrait in such a soap opera of a situation, but it's good to be ready to be tested. It wasn't my self-esteem as a marketing whiz and CEO that kept me from dissolving into a frightened and defeated heap on the luxurious Helmsley Hotel bed. It was those interior qualities I'd come to rely on— my back-against-the-wall survivor bravery, an acceptance that being in charge included tough challenges, and that my "family" (Tatham) had achieved much. All this gave me the courage to take a stand, not only for my agency, but for myself.

Your portrait allows the wisdom and wishes of your heart to infuse and then magnify the intellectual, high-performance side of you. True, deeply felt self-knowledge is the key to unlocking your best and strongest self at work. This is what underlies the emotional intelligence that lets you empathize with and motivate others. It's also the source of the vaunted charisma we all wish to project as women in charge.

How do we arrive at the office clothed in pure, unshakable self-confidence? With a self-portrait of higher expectations. You make your portrait from the inside out in order to take all of you, your wishes, your beliefs, and your passions, to work.

When you integrate all that you've uncovered, you will find a new set of priorities. There was only one woman in all my classes who chose to make only the after portrait; the others all needed to make a before and an after. Before is diagnostic, zeroing in on any problems or omissions; a trait or a message that is out of control, or neglected. The after is a full view of who you are becoming as you present your potential.

Now you and your portrait are prepared for any battle, anticipating victory.

II

PUBLIC

5

ROAD SHOW

Who They Think You Are

In 2002 CARLY Fiorina took her glamorous big-time show on the road to the executive women's conference hosted by *Fortune* magazine. Carly earned the spotlight as the keynote speaker because she had crashed through the ceiling of a Fortune 500 company when she became CEO of Hewlett-Packard.

As her remarks soon revealed, what was uppermost in Carly's mind was establishing that she was the right leader to guide HP through a challenging new era. But we women in her audience saw her as our poster girl, proof that women could run giant companies that had been the exclusive turf of men. There was a portrait mismatch between how her audience saw her and the image she wanted to project. It was severe enough to alter the reception she received.

Carly was speaking to an audience of other women stars in the working world. Everywhere I saw name tags with titles like "Group VP Manufacturing" and "Hospital Director" and "College President" and "Senior Partner." Even a short time ago, we executive women made up a small, battle-tested band of pioneers. At this conference, I was witnessing the long promised explosion of women moving to the top, in all their vibrant colors. The room was almost levitating as we came together that first morning, having arrived, each from her own perilous journey, intact and elated to be together, and delighted to celebrate one of us who had hit the big time.

As Carly walked out to a big round of applause, her very first words set the tone. "Oh, I should just mention," she said, as though she wanted to get a small issue out of the way. "I don't think it's helpful or interesting to discuss how it is that *women* lead, as I am often asked to do. I don't think of how I do this job as a woman, but as a CEO." I've paraphrased this, but it was clear to me she was saying that at work, she saw herself as a leader first and a woman second.

Carly paused, preparing to get into the body of her speech. In that silence I could feel the hush that comes at being surprised, blindsided really, by Carly's opening disclaimer. I watched as a couple of women got up and walked out of the room. In protest? I wondered.

During the coffee break, I heard women reviewing Carly's statement that she saw herself as a gender-neutral leader because for them, she was not just another CEO; she was their iconic woman leader. "Why deny that?" they were saying.

I spoke the next day. I came to the conference in my role as an undersecretary of state in the midst of war, Afghanistan and Iraq looming. I admitted it was long, lonely work, nearly friendless. The politics were harsher than the so-called tough world of big business. I realized I had actually been starving for the company of women. As I put it in my closing remarks, "It's wonderful to be here, to be with my own kind." I was probably revealing more than I intended, but part of my self-portrait those days would have included a sense of isolation, of real longing for the open world of marketing and these women I considered to be my kindred spirits. I choked up a bit when I concluded that, nevertheless, it is a great privilege to be asked to serve our country.

At that, the audience stood and applauded. I knew this was an expression of support for our country more than for me personally. Feeling like an outsider in government, I wanted to be seen (and included) as a woman first, an undersecretary second.

Carly was not speaking to us alone. She had, I think, many other audiences in mind: her board, her shareholders, the dissenting groups in her company. For both of us, that experience on stage was an interesting lesson in what happens when you and your self-portrait hit the road, encountering audiences who could be holding a different portrait of who they think you are, and above all, who they want you to be.

Showtime

The most striking reality about taking your portrait on the road versus your private portrait rehearsals is that your audience can exhibit a rude tendency to make a snap judgment about you, sizing you up based on very brief exposure; judging how well you strut

> Armed with a clearer self-knowledge, you are now ready to take your show on the road, before many audiences, to see how well your portrait travels.

your stuff. Rejection can be cruel and quick. Some Broadway shows close after opening night. Some last for years. Usually your reception will fall between these two extremes.

You are now far better prepared for a long, successful run. Your lines will come naturally from the center of your own integrity; you will move with the assurance that comes from having taken a full inventory of what you have to offer.

Now . . . about those audiences. Since your audience is carrying its own preconceived idea of who you are, how you are received will be strongly shaded by who the audience wants you to be. The more you know about all the images and expectations that your various audiences are already holding, the smarter and more successful your road show will be. The only way to find out is to ask, but this kind of more intimate "consumer" research requires a fail-safe and road-tested technique.

Your Portrait, Their View

No one will ever comprehend your complete, layered, and multi-dimensional self-portrait. That full portrait is your personal guide, something you can refer to whenever you've got a question about how you should respond to someone or react to a situation at work. It's a great tool to have at those moments when you stop seeing clearly, or when things come to a screeching halt and your shiny new sense of self runs smack into the very different picture others may have of you.

Some self-portraits have deep and broad qualities that can be presented in so many different ways it is easy to adapt to what is wanted and still get you where you want to go. Others contain a quality that, though true, may not be admirable in the world at large, but important to a particular audience. "Chainsaw Al Dunlap" was a man renowned for his ability to cut costs by swiftly and savagely reducing excess tasks, people, or entire divisions. His label makes me wince, but it got him hired over and over again. His self-portrait matched what the companies were looking for. What he presented of who he was, and what the companies saw as his unique and desirable quality, matched perfectly.

ALICE HITS A MISMATCH

Not long after completing our workshop, Alice discovered how she was seen by her boss, at a meeting of her company's area managers. Such meetings can be a great source of consumer research.

The CEO went around the room acknowledging those regions that had taken on big nationwide projects. Alice and her group were hoping to be given one of these prestigious assignments soon. When the CEO got to Alice, he said, with an approving smile, "Well, Alice, you're the best . . . well, you just do whatever we ask of you."

He meant that as a compliment, but Alice had to duck her head so her fellow managers, who were nodding in agreement, couldn't witness her dismay.

Before she had constructed her new self-portrait, Alice might have been pleased at this assessment. But she no longer wanted to be seen as the great accommodator. In our seminar, she had developed a bigger self-portrait that could guide her to be a bolder actor;

to initiate, not accommodate. Alice wondered if everyone she worked with was still running the old movie of what makes Alice run. Who her boss thought she was (when he thought about it at all), and how he wanted her to be to fit his own goals, no longer matched the new self-portrait Alice had created for herself. You'll notice that being wonderfully compliant threatens no one; that's why everyone in the meeting nodded in support. Alice knew her boss's assessment of her was outdated, but until she heard it stated so starkly, she hadn't realized how big the gap was between his view and her new, stronger, truer self-image.

This problem is not unique to Alice. It happens to all of us. Your self-portrait may not match up with how your boss or your client views you. Determining just how far apart these two pictures are calls for some dedicated research on your part.

The Qualities That Matter Most to You

As you prepare to do some "consumer" research, you should know what you're looking for. Does every kind word you hear please you? Well, it shouldn't. You are not looking for praise; you are trying to hear if others see in you the qualities you want to be known for.

Once I added the important qualities of having good judgment and carefully gathering information to go along with my drive to "be in charge," I felt I could measure up as a leader. But without those qualities, I could run things into the ground. My new portrait, "woman upon her trusty steed," embodied a promise of thoughtful change. I had to learn to moderate my tendencies to be impatient and rash, or I would be rated as unpredictable, an aspect of impatience I wanted to shed. Ultimately I earned a reputation for being good at turnarounds as "change agent."

I became known as someone who could see problems, knit solutions together, and then sell the audience on those changes. That change agent label was a match to the kind of work that most fascinated me. If no changes were needed in a company, I felt restless and disinterested.

Not an ideal way to be, but I accepted this about myself, and more importantly, I found a way to communicate that to others. So in doing my portrait research, I wasn't looking for descriptors such as thoughtful and meticulous (though these are great qualities) because I knew I could not claim them.

Choosing the key qualities that you want to emerge from your self-portrait is a serious choice. Remember, it doesn't have to be a "good" quality. Impatience does not appear on anyone's list of most desirable traits, but it was my trait and I had to claim it. I tried to shape it into a quality of being unafraid to act, of being decisive. But I could never expect to hear that I have, say, a calm demeanor. So when you say, "These are the qualities I wish to present," you are also saying, "but those are not."

Our goal in this research is to uncover how others perceive of you and the way you work. You want to know what they think of your work skills, but most of all, how they view your delivery system, your special characteristics, and your way of handling relationships. You'll never know the whole image they hold of you unless you are willing to ask.

> I'm going to give you a system for conducting sophisticated consumer research that will allow you to ask smartly and safely.

How much do you know about your reputation? All too many women say, "I'd rather not know. I'll just concentrate on doing superior work." Indeed, learning how people see you can be disturbing. Even high praise can affect your behavior in a manipulative way. But once you are grounded by your own hard-earned self-knowledge, with your self-portrait firmly in mind, you are ready to do this research.

It's Not an Evaluation, It's Research

The women I teach, whether they attend my workshops or I meet them when I'm consulting for a company, do not love hearing they are must probe into the feelings of various people at work to learn about themselves. "You mean I'm going to have to ask these turkeys what they think of me? I'd rather die than invite them to savage me openly," was one modest reaction to this consumer research assignment.

Others don't get to define you. You are simply doing research, gathering insights, impressions, stories, and fragments. Consider whatever you hear to be clues about how others view your delivery of your work and important information about what your company wants from you. Sometimes you'll even get a surprising window into who *they* are.

Here's your safety net: remember that no matter what you hear in the interview it is not the whole truth of who you are.

There's an important difference between this consumer research and a typical job evaluation. Your company's evaluation system can be helpful in terms of how well you're performing, but we are interested in how well you're communicating *all* of who you are. In our research, we are investigating their full perception of you. These answers are more insightful, pinpointing what is distinctive and unique in the way you work.

Evaluations are rating systems about measurable work skills that are readily assessed. When evaluations dwell on descriptions of work style, they become vague or repeat buzz talk such as "Own your leadership" or "Have more presence" or "Instill belief." What do you do when you hear such comments? Feel vaguely uneasy, I'd imagine.

The 360 degree review now widely used in industry evaluations intends to report on your standing from a wide array of audiences—the top, side, and bottom. When they are anonymous, they can do great harm because they can provide an invitation to attack, to vent, to make an assessment without accountability or dialogue. A woman doctor I know, who headed a department at a teaching hospital, had her relationship with her direct reports destroyed by a 360 degree review. The anonymous comments were so personal, irrelevant, and mean-spirited that there was no going back to working well together. You are doing your own research, but you hold a compass—your self-portrait. The intention expressed by your self-portrait is your reference point for this research. It helps to know that you are searching for validation of certain qualities and ways you want to be seen.

> You are not worried about popularity or approval or any feedback that doesn't apply to your own portrait goals.

Alice's research came after she had already begun to practice getting out of the floodplain where everyone was "irrigating off her waters." She was expressing her bigger self-portrait as a mighty river with strong boundaries, and she controlled the current.

She started to say no and took firm steps to hold department chiefs to schedules and called in people to weekend work rather than doing it herself. Her "consumers" were puzzled and cross: "You're rather impatient now, so quick to judge me." "You didn't even ask us; you just did it."

Alice was delighted; her new, firmer boundaries were showing. "You know," she said, "people don't like it when you cut off their water. This period of disruption is inevitable. I'm right on target."

How to Survey the Way They See You

Begin by choosing carefully the person you will interview and by learning how to approach this unusual kind of research.

Who: Pick people who are key players in your work life, including competitors. Don't just pick the ones you know well. However, juniors are a great source of unfiltered impressions. For key people not easily available, you must take the initiative and find a way, if necessary, to meet outside of work.

Rehearse: Practice on people you trust or know well until you get a sense of how the questions flow. You'll learn not to feel uneasy about the myriad answers you may receive. Practice how to be objective and consider how to probe beyond the first obvious answers. You are a researcher, not a supplicant.

Approach: Set up an informal session without flagging it as something your interviewee has to be alarmed about or prepare for. (You'd be amazed at how bosses will scurry to get opinions on someone who asks for a "review." If they don't know much, that tells you there's a different kind of gap in their portrait of you.) Tell them you are interested in their perceptions of you. Add that this is an informal discussion for your own understanding; it's your private project. You can add something like, "You are someone I feel I can trust to help me evaluate how I'm perceived at work. I'm not looking for praise or asking you for anything specific, but to open a dialogue."

Subject: Ask about your work skills (how you get the job done) and then how they think you deliver the work. Define this as your relationship with others, your attitude, and other qualities you bring to your work. Ask if they have any other opinions about your work style or behavior.

Begin the conversation with how your candidate views your work skills; this is familiar territory. But a discussion about all the ways you deliver the work is where you learn how others identify what makes you tick: what sort of portrait they're holding and how multidimensional or one-sided it is.

Always ask for an example: It is possible to expand on even a generic descriptor such as "smart" (almost everyone is rated as smart) by asking, "Can you give me an example?" Whenever your candidate mentions a characteristic that captures your attention, use the magic of this question: "Can you give me an example?" It's in the examples that the important clues are found.

Notice in Sandy's interview with her boss how she learns the most interesting facts *only* after she asks him to give her an example.

SANDY: How would you say I approach the work?

BOSS: Well, Sandy, you are always well prepared.

SANDY: What's an example of that?

BOSS: You always have everything thoroughly done, well prepared.

SANDY: Can you give me an example?

BOSS: Well, like that report on how we should evaluate opportunities for new acquisitions.

SANDY: Is that an example of being well prepared?

BOSS: Well, yes, but I don't recall you ever asked me for input.

SANDY: Was that a good thing? (She's catching on that there's more here.)

BOSS: As a matter of fact, no. I did have some thoughts on it.

SANDY: Is that an example of being too prepared?

BOSS: As a matter of fact, Sandy, you do tend to come in with the cake already baked.

That was the Aha! moment for Sandy.

Sandy's boss would not have given her this insight if she hadn't pressed him in a nonjudgmental way. Because she did, she learned, in one unforgettable phrase, that he was not always so pleased with her tendency to gather all the ingredients, mix, and bake the cake without help from him or others.

Now Sandy knows exactly what she needs to do. She has learned it's not necessary to prove she can do it all. She knows she should allow other voices to influence when and how she completes her task, especially voices that come from the top.

> Sandy is communicating something important: that this is an objective exercise for her.

Notice Sandy is not reacting as she and her boss talk. She's registering what he's saying, maybe even writing it down. The more neutral her reactions, the more her boss will relax and reveal how he really feels. There's another important technique here. When Sandy says, "Is that an example of being well prepared?" she repeats his exact words.

Hint: Repeat the Revealing Comment

I didn't learn the strategy of circling back and repeating what was heard when I was a consumer research supervisor at Uncle Ben's Rice. Rather, I learned it when I observed a two-day workshop for couples conducted by Rick Brown, director of the Relationships Therapy Institute. I was curious to see if this kind of couple's communication, more intimate, more intense, called for different ways of communicating than I'd been taught in the advertising business. A pair of nuns made up the only non–male-female couple in the group.

TWO PEOPLE TALKING

An exacting technique is needed when two people in a close relationship try to exchange information, because there is a high probability of tension, emotion, and even willful misunderstanding. Sounds like your prospective consumer research with your boss or your competitor, doesn't it?

Rick asked the ten pairs to find a separate place in the open studio to begin their first exercise. One person in each couple was to speak to the other about an issue that was important to them both. Then the partner was to repeat exactly what the other person said. It was this simple: "What I heard you say was . . . " In every case the woman started first. To my surprise, this exchange seemed to take forever.

I was amazed that almost none of the women found the first echo of their remarks satisfactory. If they noticed their partner was rephrasing what they said or substituting a word, that really got a veto.

That's an important discipline for your interview too. For instance, Sandy needed to use the term "well prepared" and not add to or redefine what her boss said. In research you don't want to expand on someone's thinking by adding your interpretation. Your job is to record the opinion, ask for an example, and double back by repeating exactly what was said.

With the couples, things got more complicated when the man was asked to describe in his own words what he thought his partner meant. All around the room, women began shaking their heads. One woman burst into tears of frustration as she talked to her red-faced partner. It's a good thing the nuns were there; they were the only calm pair in the room.

That exercise demonstrates how hard it is to be accurately heard or correctly interpreted. It wasn't that the listening partner was obtuse or stubborn; it was that he spontaneously filtered what was said through his own memories and biases, automatically adding his own opinions and feelings. One of the couples had the added disadvantage of not knowing each other well, since they'd only recently become engaged. At the end of the two days, the woman decided to leave her lover at the altar. She understood finally what he was saying and realized they were not a match.

> Double back and repeat an exact phrase as a question in your review.

Try it; double back when you hear a revealing comment. We don't naturally do this because we're afraid of being seen as slow on the uptake, but it's important to risk repetition in your research. It's like breathing oxygen into the tension that can arise when you ask people to tell you what they feel about you.

RACHEL HEARS TOO MUCH

Rachel got positive feedback for being Little Red Riding Hood, saving others, making peace. People wanted her to stay in the fairy tale, mediating between the wolf and Grandma, although it was no longer the picture she wanted for herself. She did her consumer research over dinner with two key clients. At first, it was a love fest. "They called me the center of everything, they felt my intensity, and they appreciated how I could bring everyone back together when dissension arose. Since they emphasized how much I cared, I decided that would be my double back question."

"So you feel I care a lot about the business?" she asked, expecting the same reassurance, but then they looked at each other and one added, *"Actually, you care so much that you tend to take things too personally."* The other chimed in, *"Way too personally."*

"This took me by surprise, and I was so mad I forgot to stay in neutral. All I could think was, Screw you. After all those hours I'd spent putting back together what they kept pulling apart."

At dinner, Rachel uncovered a facet of how she delivered her work that she didn't like, but after thinking it over, she felt much clearer.

> *I do care a lot. That's really how I got the peacemaker label. I intend to alter the weak side of that image. I want to be seen as responsible for making important change, but right now, they see me as so caring, they feel protective, afraid I'll be crushed, weeping in a corner. But I know I can handle any strife. That was a very mind-opening comment. What if I'd missed that?*

The Question of Significance

To deliver on our promise to Ogilvy clients to understand the relationship between a product and its users in our consumer research, we developed something we called the "significance question." This is the big gun you use when you need to get a deeper understanding of something you've been told in your research. The question is the same one you used to open Pandora's Box. Here we use it as, "What is the significance of 'that' comment to you?"

This takes the interview out of its logical flow, asking the responder to think in a broader context and give you an answer that may be completely out of left field. It gives you a chance to learn something new. At the very least, you force someone like your boss out of guarded business-speak evaluations.

Color Is Significant

The significance question can open up a new dimension whenever you pose it. I had an account team at Ogilvy who thought this new way of doing consumer research, by asking the consumer the significance of a certain opinion, was way too much like therapy.

Morris said to me, "Really, Charlotte, what's the emotional hook? How deeply can you feel about your moving truck?" He had us all laughing because his client was Ryder truck rentals, and he knew both Ryder and its main competitor, U-Haul, very well. Reluctantly he agreed to ask The Question.

Morris came back to my office with a dove of peace taped to the cover of a research report. "I still can't believe it," he said, tapping the report. "We asked, 'What's the significance of Ryder Trucks in your life when you're thinking of making a move?' I expected them to hoot with laughter. These were some tough guys. They said, 'Yellow.' I didn't catch on at first; then they helped me out. 'Ryder trucks are shiny yellow. U-Haul is gray, kinda secondhand looking.' I tell you, the Ryder people were very grateful to learn that because they were considering eliminating the high-grade yellow finish as a way to cut costs."

> How-they-see-you research is not just probing for flaws; it's also hunting for treasure.

In the discussions, you may find something precious you didn't know you should be emphasizing. We were all surprised to discover that the color of Ryder trucks helped distinguish them, even made them more fun to drive. If we hadn't asked that question, we'd never have unearthed the power of shiny yellow over drab gray. Such an emotional response would never have come up in standard consumer research.

Margo Interviews a Competitor

In your personal consumer research, you may come upon an interview that feels like a personal attack; after all, you'll be surveying rivals as well as peers. You can stop this kind of interview pronto by saying, "Thank-you. That was very interesting." Or you can bring out the big gun by asking, "What's the significance of that?" Here's how it played out for Margo:

> HOSTILE COWORKER: Frankly, I think you're overly competitive and we're supposed to be a team here.
> MARGO: What's an example of that?
> COWORKER: Well, you seemed to take all the credit for that last big order from IBM.
> MARGO: What's the significance of that to you?
> COWORKER: Well . . . it's hard on the team. Also, I guess I felt left out.

In this last statement, Margo learned more about her coworker than she did about herself. It's true her boss had singled out Margo in a meeting for this sales win, but Margo didn't lobby to get herself named as the star player. She didn't think this discussion added much to her own portrait research, but she had a much clearer idea of how sensitive her coworker was to her place in the team. That's useful information too.

Research Turns Up Treasures

Thelma's research helped her reorder her own view of herself, with only one added comment. At first, she was all over the place with far too much miscellaneous information from her interviews. That picture of confusion was reflected in her before portrait.

BEFORE PORTRAIT

I AM IN THE HAMSTER'S WHEEL.
I exhaust myself (and everyone else) running here and there.

Her research revealed that others saw her as positive, intelligent, intimidating, while she saw herself as team player, focused, brainy. There was not much overlap between her picture and theirs. She admitted, "I found the whole process confusing and depressing until I did the research interview with Jed."

Jed was the top account director and her boss. Thelma's creative gifts had recently gotten her promoted to be supervisor of a team in a company that designs logos, packaging, and uniforms.

JED: You deliver the work in your own fierce, frantic sort of way.

THELMA: What's an example of that?

JED: Well, when our hotel chain client was startled by your design work and terrified by your intensity in presenting it.

THELMA: What's the significance of that? (Feeling more and more like a scared hamster.)

JED: You are the brave one; you will pull us all out of a rut into fresh modern design.

THELMA: Oh my God.

Jed's comment showed Thelma where she needed to go—she really was a fiery and edgy creative talent. She could quit running in circles and start steering her team to a whole new level of breakthrough design. Now she had her after portrait.

AFTER PORTRAIT

I AM A CAPTAIN
I take the wheel, guiding the boat.

How Jed saw her led her to add this phrase to her captain's role:

"Through uncharted waters of great beauty."

Monitoring Your Reactions

Be prepared to be confused by dumb remarks or half-truths you may hear during your interviews. This is not the time to defend yourself or debate the points. Just take it all in.

Step Back

It's important to step way back from feelings of resentment and hurt and observe the picture of yourself that you've just received. Turn it this way and that. Examine it for resonance, look for things you need to learn. Then you can decide what to do.

Never allow negative reviews, remarks, or what seem to be false pictures to alter who you are at the center. Others do not get to re-invent you. But you need to pay attention to negative reviews. Regard them as a wake-up call, a cold splash of water on your face.

It helps to know that after you've done your research, you'll go through three reactions (we all do).

Defend

You will react first by defending, revisiting, and explaining to every-one (especially yourself) what the real circumstances are. That's a lot better than falling over and saying, "Go ahead, walk on me."

One of our women stammered in dismay when I used the "walk on me" reference. It triggered an uneasy memory. "Oh my God, I just did that, only worse," she said. "Charlie told me I was chosen for the an-nual award as the most all-around productive salesman. I said, 'Me? Wasn't there anyone else more qualified?'"

She had just reinforced her before image of being modest, maybe unworthy. I wanted to send her back to portrait school. She needed to correct the image she had given her boss. To do that, she'd need to discover where that image was coming from and why it wasn't valid. Step back and watch out for out-of-focus pictures.

Observe

You will need to look objectively at the other, possibly blurry pictures that appear. My first boss at Uncle Ben's Rice put me on probation, saying I was distracted, receiving flowers at the office, getting too many phone calls. I didn't think probation sounded so lethal, but then he showed me just how big the gap was between his perception and my reality, by promoting my good friend, Patsy, to the next rung. I spent many nights explaining to myself why I was qualified, in fact more qualified than Patsy. And she was my friend! Then I got real: Patsy was ready and it showed. There was a reason I'd been put on probation. It was like getting a head-clearing whack. I dropped the frivolous young puppy profile (that's actually what they called me at the office) I'd been projecting and got to work.

Act

Be prepared to change your delivery system, but never offer to change your essential portrait. Even after my probation at Uncle Ben's, I never once thought I shouldn't qualify for and go after promotions. I felt I had to do a visible about-face. So I gave my boss a two-page list of tests I had set for myself and asked him to judge me on these new, tough criteria. Over time, I found my view of him changed remarkably. He was a tough boss, but he also pushed me in a good way. In time, I was given a big promotion, leaping over others to the exalted position of product manager. You would have thought it was his promotion. He went around beaming and shaking hands with the team that picked me. I think he saw a much bigger, better Charlotte than I did, and he shoved me into trying that on for size. I never thanked Morgan properly for putting me on probation and then pushing me along the path; that probation was one of my earliest pieces of consumer research.

Survey Size

You can conduct interviews one-on-one or with a group. You can also learn a lot indirectly by paying attention to clues and getting into the habit of calling back after meetings or key events to ask what someone thought. Always focus on your delivery system, not the work.

When Thelma heard that her intensity had scared her client, the hotel chain director, she was tipped off to call and ask him how he thought the last meeting went. The call itself seemed to please him; it wasn't typical for the creative supervisor to call. Then he told her about the reaction of others to the work. He ended by saying, "We don't always know what you're talking about, you're so fast, but no one doubts your talent or your conviction."

"Whew," Thelma responded. "I think I can slow down now. They hear me."

> Researching one-to-one sets up a whole different dynamic.

I believe in one-on-one interviews for most of your research. You are asking for some emotionally charged information, and when you can create intimacy and trust in a private one-on-one interview, it's valuable. It can feel risky to open yourself up to criticism or personal reviews.

Rachel would have had a much better time of it had she interviewed only one client rather than having to watch two clients exchanging glances.

It's always a good idea to meet away from the work setting, for drinks or coffee, especially for a one-on-one with a higher-level audience. It sets a relaxed tone and makes the whole endeavor more fun. Remember not to telegraph your intentions by giving the candidates a big setup or long advance notice. It's fair to say you want to catch them off their guard. At least try to keep things informal. You are not conducting an inquisition.

Group Research: A Slow Walk Together

Men seem to favor indirect research. A lot of men who worked for me wouldn't ask a direct question of me or anyone else. Rather, they'd jump right to asking for the next position on the ladder. Of course, that request often forced a discussion of their capabilities.

Men have a very effective way of doing their research. It's called golf. I have a lot of respect for this approach. Men have other sports and games, but ever since I was a green account exec on the fringe of a group listening to the big man at Gillette describe a certain golf course in South America, I've been mystified by the long hours devoted to following the little white ball. It seemed to require a staggering commitment of time to little purpose. Then I finally understood that was the point; golf is one way to have a long, slow walk together. It's not networking in the sense of lobbying or exchanging favors.

> Look for an indirect way to learn what a person or group of people think of you, as well as a chance to present who you are.

What golf is really about was made vividly clear early in my tenure as CEO of Ogilvy. I was dismayed when I learned that our second board meeting had been scheduled in some obscure corner of Scotland. It was St. Andrews, perhaps the most famous links in the world.

At dinner the first night, I witnessed how this board of eighteen people (Shelly Lazarus and I were the only nongolfers) had come through a very rocky period at Ogilvy still at ease with one another. It was the ease that comes from having taken many long walks together. It wasn't necessarily based on friendship; I knew there were warring factions among them. The Germans disagreed with the Brits' approach and they were all leery of the Americans, but there was a degree of mutual respect and a keen awareness of what they could expect from one another. Every golf trip extended their knowledge in an indirect but accurate way. This familiarity and level of trust would serve us very well in the bumpy months to come as we performed some aggressive surgery on Ogilvy's portrait.

Their Stick Figure View

It's easier to interview people who know you pretty well, who have worked with you and watched you and had a chance to experience key aspects of who you are. But here's a word of warning. Even they will usually not hold the multifaceted, many-layered image you'd hope for. The higher you go for your interviews, the less nuanced their picture of you will be.

I've seen the reports from the bosses. They usually contain two assessments: one quality they'd like to see improved and one quality that impresses them.

> You learn that the people holding your career in their hands prefer to keep it simple.

Even important women in good positions are often described by their bosses with a simplistic word picture like "mother hen." Once or twice in our workshops, a woman would apply "mother hen" to herself to indicate a protective, nurturing quality in her way of working. That always made me feel a little anxious for her. And I hated to read that description in a boss's comments. The term implies that the woman is not leadership material. With this metaphor, the boss is saying that this woman clucks about her chicks, teaching and watching over them. And believe me, you'll never hear a boss say, "Hey, we need a mother hen to get this division going."

At Tatham, I was once reduced to a label, but simplistic as it was, it was a whopper of a piece of consumer research. Our client, Oscar Mayer, asked us to do some role-playing to get at what we really did beyond our titles. After the facilitator had thoroughly investigated our roles at work, he pointed straight at me. "What would you say she does?" he asked the group.

"She's the interrupter," several of them said at once, and they all broke out in pleased laughter. They were so proud of nailing me that I blushed. But it's true. CEOs do interrupt a lot, and one like me, whose traits are impatience and being in charge, is likely to be a serial interrupter. This version of my portrait rose up to bite me. I left that meeting thinking perhaps I should listen more and occasionally yield the floor.

All day long, if you pay attention, you'll get feedback on how others see you. Often the portraits they paint are oversimplified, but they still give you clues as to how you are seen and how you've been delivering the work.

We live in a marketplace that seeks to eliminate complexity. This leaves little room to express the soft stuff, like passion and trustworthiness, the glue to relationships.

Everyone will revert to the simplicity of a label if you let them. When President Bush called himself the "decider," the press used it everywhere; at last, a label. When the foreign press in Washington, D.C., wanted to diminish me, they called me the "Madison Avenuer."

Though your manager may have only a snapshot or a stick figure outline of you, he or she is still assessing you. "They" includes everyone over you, the "deciders" in your organization. The life they can change is yours.

Without a Portrait, Managers Guess

Many women are lulled into believing that management will see deeply into who they are and come to a fair and positive estimate of something as elusive as their potential. Don't believe it. Only you can assess and communicate your potential, and to do so effectively, you do need to know how they see you.

> It's nearly impossible for a workplace to be a meritocracy, even when those in charge wish it could be.

Don't assume that the workplace is a meritocracy, that you will be given rewards commensurate with your work, your dedication, your long hours. Though managers would prefer to reward and rank people based on objective measures such as performance, results, effort, and good work habits, it often doesn't happen that way. It's a subjective process, and people are sometimes moved ahead for some really off the charts reasons.

Not necessarily typical, but instructive, was a comment from Dolores, who owns a real estate company. She explained to me that she had lost a huge land development deal after a solid year of work. We were working on how she engages others, so I asked, "What part of the relationship fell apart?"

"Oh," she answered casually, "the other agent, my rival, is sleeping with him." That's one way to change . . . or kill a meritocracy.

The workplace is an emotional arena, where fear, jealousy, sex, resentment, and bias often rule. It is a place where many people dance to someone else's tune, however off-key it may be.

I know how managers use their picture of you to make decisions because I've been in these meetings. When we managers meet (the bigger the job opportunity, the fewer will be in the room), we don't really focus on the work. We spend about five minutes on how well various contenders do the job. Managers know all of the candidates do good work, so how hard and how well a person works is rarely a tiebreaker.

What's more important are the intangible assets people bring to the work and the qualities they are known for. These delivery qualities can include energy, goodwill, drive, or judgment, charm, loyalty, independence, curiosity, among others. Companies develop a private code for what they want to see in their winners. My client at Gillette felt, "Everyone around here has brains. I'm looking for tenacity." At Procter & Gamble, the kiss of death was to be seen as "lacking good judgment." Do you know what qualities your company prizes? That is the lens through which they will view you.

Since these intangible qualities are rarely supported by "proof," evaluators have to rely on speculation to make their case. The discussion strays to a mix of office stories, gossip, rumors, and tales of victory or defeat. It's not very exact, but managers have no choice. We must assess who's in there.

> The more multidimensional the picture managers have of you, the better it is for you.

Your current performance has gotten you into the running. Now we managers are trying to read how you will handle a whole new set of circumstances, so we have to become amateur psychologists, guessers, and estimators. Helping your managers read you is a matter of self-defense.

Bosses send me comments about women with whom I'll be working. After a page of praise, they boil everything down to one issue to be addressed or one key attribute of that person's delivery system. It is just such summations you can uncover in your research.

There's rarely mention of the work itself. These assessments are all about delivery. Comments like "radiates confidence," "gets steamrolled," "dodges the ugly stuff," "ice cold" are the snapshots managers use to evaluate you. Some of these inexact impressions call for a dramatic change in your delivery style or ask you to expand them so that your portrait is accurately seen.

Now that you know more about how you're perceived at work, having asked smartly, objectively, and bravely about such an intimate, emotional, and elusive subject, you are in a position of power. You can concentrate on how to put your biggest aspirations for yourself into their evolving picture of you.

That's your road show, the one destined for a long successful run.

Story: External Action

The lessons I took from my time as CEO of Ogilvy Advertising helped frame the lessons from this next section of the book. Tatham was a story of an intensive investigation of "the stranger within." At Ogilvy I learned how to present what I believed I had to offer. My road show was not to be a smooth one.

After the press announced that I was leaving Tatham, I received three huge job offers, all CEO level, from agencies ten times the size of Tatham, spread all over the world and . . . in trouble. It was a time of turmoil in these giant multinational agencies, accused of being fat and slow, even though to my eye, they held astonishing resources and a mouthwatering big-name client list. I benefited from the notoriety of leading a (rare for those days) successful Tatham revitalization.

Martin Sorrell, chairman of the holding company WPP, which now owned Ogilvy, posed the most tempting offer. It was the chairman/CEO position at Ogilvy, but while all my suitors were looking for transformation, Ogilvy's famous but faded history of building great brands was the tiebreaker for me.

Ogilvy was having a tough time, losing flagship clients like American Express and Ponds, plus key people, profits, and most of all, confidence. We still had American Express in Europe, though it was shaky and run by an infamous bully who did not love Ogilvy. At the conclusion of a big presentation that took six months of preparation from our offices in Spain, Germany, and England the bully simply said, "We won't comment today. We'll get back to you." It was a slap in the face. As the demoralized Ogilvy team silently began folding up charts, I spoke up; I'm afraid my anger was as audible as my words. "Well, I'll comment. I'm still a neutral party and I want to tell you how stunningly good this work seems to me and why." The Amex team couldn't resist jumping in and next steps were agreed on. Bully boy smoldered.

It was easy for me to rise up and blunt the bully; I was defending great work and good people. But it wasn't clear that I could be so sure-footed amid the complex international turf issues at Ogilvy nor with our many far-flung clients.

The press did not hesitate to trumpet how little international experience I had, and my board, eighteen world managers from Europe to Asia, was eyeing me with polite skepticism.

I decided the only way I would be seen as qualified to lead was to gather immediate, legitimate, high-level intel. I set up meetings with thirty-one of our top clients. Not one refused me, one benefit of the landslide press I'd received about being the "first woman to crash through the glass ceiling." They were curious. I asked for one-on-one meetings because I couldn't risk the normal process of getting to know such clients in group meetings over the years. Our changes needed to come fast and smart and be highly visible.

I got a glimpse of how far I was from home (and comfort) in rainy Vevey, Switzerland. The urbane head of Nestlé, in our stroll to the dining room, turned to his assistant and asked, "And what language will lunch be in?"

I interrupted, "Well, I hope it's in Texan, because that's my specialty."

I felt my first Ogilvy board meeting, scheduled to meet in Vienna, would set my future relationship with the top people. But at the meeting, there was such a chorus of dissenting voices, all equally loud, that I wondered how I would ever find a way to be heard, to take the lead. As I entered the long, forbidding room, I was distressed to see twelve-inch-thick board books at each seat. I could feel my chance to redirect our focus getting lost in a litany of regional issues, dreary financial numbers, and endless detail involving the management of eight thousand people. Then a lovely thing happened. As I pulled out my chair at the head, my big red book teetered and fell to the floor with a loud, satisfying bang. It gave me courage. "Leave it." I was clear now. "That's not what we're doing today."

I began an hour-long presentation, without notes, about what our top clients had to say about Ogilvy. Every word of the ten-hour meeting that followed was a forced march into reality. Shelly Lazarus, then the head of New York, later remembered, "It was like being in a Fellini movie. We were in this old castle and all the rules were being broken; people were unnerved and exhilarated."

My ace in the hole was that I could tell these veterans something even they didn't know, because I had asked each client in those intimate meetings (after we got past the recital of the failings of Ogilvy) what kept them awake at night. Their real-life answers allowed me to respond in kind, and I had a deeper understanding of our clients I could share with the Oglivy team.

Every day, with every step I made, I had to present who I was and what I believed in. I got some of it right. In a video sent worldwide, I reminded us all that David Ogilvy, our founder, had not given us his beautiful company values as a foundation on which to rest but to reinvent ourselves passionately and on a daily basis. To illustrate, I challenged one of David's famous sayings. "We prefer gentlemen with brains." I could hear them laughing, but I made an unexpected point. "I do not object to the word 'gentlemen' because of gender—as you might have noticed, this is obviously obsolete. I object because the phrase seems to favor being polite over a zest for the work . . . and by the way, brains are a given."

I got some of it wrong too. The ultimate legacy for any CEO begins every morning at 8:00 AM, when she chooses what to do that day from among all the pressing problems and pressures on her desk. The days move so swiftly and your choices prove either right or wrong much later. My choices were to attract new work from our multinationals and woo back recently lost clients. I was looking for the shortest distance to new revenue for Ogilvy. I kept missing the mandated WPP financial reviews; I was way too busy. A top WPP finance guy calmly announced they would take the finances of Ogilvy into WPP, a clear punishment for my nonattendance. I fought it, but they were adamant. I saw that I had made a big mistake in shunning the financial grind. It was a careless move on my part, a result of my infamous impatience plus my focus on growth not costs. WPP wouldn't yield, and I knew that without direct access to our own finances, we had no leverage. Late in the day, I sent in my formal resignation, just eight months after I joined Ogilvy.

There was a flurry of hushed phone calls and WPP withdrew its "offer." I never missed another financial review.

What Ogilvy needed, I soon realized, was an idea so large, so compelling, it would unite everyone and break up the defensive fiefdoms based on geography and the separate talent centers such as creative, research, or direct mail. All were clutching their self-interest rafts for safety in the storm.

I proposed we rethink brands with my concept that brands are really defined by the relationship that exists between product and user. I had studied and revered this relationship for years and knew the relationship was emotional, illogical, and full of promise. I named a "thirsty-for-change" team, made up of *people I thought had the power and the will to make a new Ogilvy (leaving out, unfortunately, some miffed bystanders). They took it from there to christen our new brand philosophy as "brand stewardship." Soon we had a well thought out process and a few client believers. But we met resistance and indifference from far too many of our offices. "It's too complicated" or "It's so obvious," they said. They'd been through too many "visions" in the last few difficult years.*

Late in year two, Business Week suggested I was in over my head. Progress had stalled, and the brand vision was limping along unsupported and losing advocates. In desperation, like a final aria, I delivered my most passionate plea for brand stewardship to a large gathering of some of our biggest clients, General Foods and Kraft among them. There were other agency heads speaking that day, but I treated it like a private dialogue, a call for help. At the end of my plea, the room rose in great agreement, clients standing, saying in every way, "I want this." Ogilvy offices received calls from these clients asking for "some brand stewardship." I had spoken for our new vision many times before, but never with so much belief and urgency. It makes a difference when your passions are in full view.

Now we had a surefire delivery system. We could woo our people through their clients, but still I feared we'd never be given the time to get around to all of them. A possible knight on a white horse appeared, but he came with a few disadvantages. We would have to forfeit $600 million in other ad billings (revenue) to play with this knight. Better known as IBM, the knight had troubles of his own.

IBM, a struggling giant, had a new CEO, Lou Gerstner. His revolutionary idea was to consolidate all the work of their fifty-plus ad agencies into corporate headquarters so they could speak with "one voice." Lou had developed his own vision to communicate. But in sprawling IBM, his vision was sure to be large and disruptive, internally as well as among its millions of users. Our price tag of $600 million was our current ad budget from clients we'd have to resign to avoid IBM conflicts—Microsoft, Compaq, and AT&T. It was terrifying, unthinkable. Yet after IBM approached us to be one of a few contestants for the prize, I thought about it every day.

When we became one of two finalists, the tension spiked at Ogilvy and WPP. "Where's the prize?" Martin Sorrell asked me, alarmed at the prospect. I could not really prove any of it, but I felt deeply this move would save Ogilvy, if it worked. We'd have an instant worldwide delivery system for brand steward-ship (which they greatly admired in the secret reviews). I felt the clients we'd have to resign were lukewarm on Ogilvy. Our company would be united in a great worthwhile venture, and I believed Lou could pull off this transformation of IBM. Here I learned the true definition of bravery; it's actually when every other safer alternative stinks. That's where I was. I felt we had to bet on this big one, and Martin finally agreed: "Well, it's on you then." Exactly.

We did win the world's largest account. The inspired Ogilvy teams came through with brilliant work, and Lou managed his own turnaround of IBM most impressively. We became once again the embodiment of David Ogilvy's dream . . . One Agency Indivisible.

During our most vulnerable period, when Ogilvy was neither ahead nor completely lost, a Harvard professor, a dark-haired beauty in stylish black high heels, appeared in my office to pursue a case study on leadership for Harvard graduate school, putting Ogilvy and Beers under scrutiny. It was terrifying to imagine failing under such an analytical eye.

Though our "thirsty for change" team eventually led the way to our unifying vision for Ogilvy, the Harvard case quote is true: "There was an amazing amount of distraction, irrelevance, and digression." All innovation and change is disruptive; only the promise of a better day will inspire others enough that they will follow.

In the teacher's notes from Case 9–495–031 is a terse confirmation of the greatest lesson I learned at Ogilvy: "Effective leaders are master communicators."

I had one great last treat coming before I left. I could hand the baton to Shelly Lazarus. Shelly shepherded Ogilvy to a whole new level of good work and pros-perity. I may have had the pioneer role, but Shelly's confident rule of Ogilvy took the question of whether women can lead right off the table.

I retired, failed retirement, and took the chairman role at my old "univer-sity," J. Walter Thompson, which was also a WPP agency. Then I received that fateful phone call from Colin Powell and became his undersecretary of state, running a department with a big charter—to build mutual understanding be-tween the United States and the rest of the world.

At the State Department, I was a total novice one day, the equivalent of a three-star general the next. There I relearned that job cycles are not stationary. We cycle in and out of different degrees of leading and following. The most intense learning curve is when you're on your knees, humbled and uncertain. "It's not how far you fall, it's how fast you recover" became my motto.

As a working woman, I learned we thrive if we can feel we are in charge, and able to inspire and influence others. We may not all aspire to be leaders at the top, but we all want to be in charge of how we represent ourselves and as much as possible, make our own way at work.

Work was so often just one presentation after another, forcing me to study what I wanted to say, how to say it, and persuasively so. That's the only road to being a "master communicator." In these years, I learned that why I was working shifted importantly. Regardless of my title, I was often meant to follow, sometimes manage, occasionally lead.

The key is not to miss that last one, when there's an opportunity for you to lead.

6

RELATIONSHIPS

Your Delivery System

EDGAR BRONFMAN JR., head of one of Ogilvy's top clients, fired me after I had been CEO of Ogilvy for only six months. I don't mean he fired the agency for our work on their brands. He fired me, personally, because of a relationship issue. I was a little far along in my career to be reminded once again that there are times when the relationship matters more than the work.

Martin Sorrell, the head of Ogilvy's holding company and my boss, called to give me the chilling news on an equally frigid Monday morning in February. "Your client felt you insulted him at the museum affair honoring his father Saturday night," Martin said. "What in the world happened?"

Months before, I had been very flattered when Leonard Lauder, the head of Estée Lauder, a man I've always admired, asked me to cochair the Whitney Museum's annual fund-raiser, which would be attended by all the big names in New York. Edgar Bronfman Sr. was being honored as a longtime contributor to the museum, along with Seagram's, the company he developed.

Though this was a prestigious nod to Ogilvy and my new position, our public relations team was worried about the pressure there'd be to help raise big money for the museum. The spotlight would be on me in what they called the "shark-infested waters of New York." But things went well; many of our clients attended this very glamorous evening and contributed generously. The day before the event, my office informed me that Edgar Bronfman Jr., whom I had not yet met, would not be attending. Odd, I thought, that Edgar Jr. would not be there, and I then forgot about it. In hindsight, I wonder how I could have been so careless.

The evening was a sellout and the table I hosted was full; the event promised to be fun. Before the first course, a panicky assistant nudged me brusquely. Edgar Bronfman Jr. and his fiancée were standing next to her, looking in vain for their proper seats at my table. I jumped up, but obviously there was no room, so we found a twosome nearby with some very elegant people whom they knew. As I watched them say hello to their table, I thought they were by far the most beautiful couple in the room.

The following Monday morning, Edgar called Martin Sorrell and fired me. He felt I had completely diminished both his company's standing at Ogilvy and his place of prestige as the honoree's son. He even told Martin Sorrell I was drunk when I made a few remarks during the program. That's how angry he was. In fact, I was probably the only person in the room who had held onto one drink all night.

This was definitely my problem to solve. I'd learned plenty of times in my career that a failure in a relationship is far more deadly than a failure to perform the work, and I was beyond exasperated with myself. I knew I had to get over to Edgar's office in the Seagram Building on Park Avenue. Normally, that splendid building, a tall black icon of modernism with its own private "lake" in front, causes me to stop and gaze in wonder. But now it loomed like the evil black tower in *Lord of the Rings*.

Though Edgar had agreed to see me, it was very rough going. He had been deeply offended and maintained a forbidding and unresponsive manner throughout the hour. There seemed to be no way to start fresh and I was about to just give up. But I felt I had to defend our agency efforts for that night. "You know Ogilvy and our clients raised over $50,000 for this benefit to honor your father. It really meant a lot to us, and we put our hearts into it," I said. At that, his whole manner changed. His posture softened. So did his tone. He'd had no idea we had all worked so hard on their behalf.

Some months later, well after the museum debacle, Edgar and I laughed about The Evening, for by then we had developed a rapport. How had I missed the very obvious point that he would be deeply affected by this event in honor of his father? Why hadn't I picked up the phone to call him when I got the misinformation that he didn't plan to attend? In New York, I learned, there is no daylight between social relationships and business relationships, but I had put all my focus on my role at this glittering social affair.

Work Relationships Are Different

By the way, even though this work relationship was emotional enough to get me fired (temporarily), it wasn't personal. That's one of the unique aspects of work relationships. They are passionate and emotional, filled with as much drama as a soap opera, but they are not personal. Clearly our female talent for connecting deeply to others and taking things personally needs to be activated differently at work.

Just as you call on a whole other set of personal qualities at work than you do at home, so the wide web of relationships at work calls for different kinds of personal qualities. It is through these relationships that you will actually deliver your after portrait.

You now have one singular advantage. Your portrait makes one relationship clear: how you relate to you. Once you've done your consumer research and have the measure of the gap between your portrait and how others assess you, you are far better prepared to build effective relationships at work.

I wish someone had given me a set of guidelines about what matters in all these contact points at work. I had to learn them one painful episode at a time. Considering how I blundered with Edgar Bronfman Jr., it's obvious that it's easy to miss that moment when the relationship takes precedence over the work, no matter how lofty your title.

There will come a time when your greatest challenge is not within the scope of the work, but is purely a matter of how you present yourself and how you engage with others. We are now at the moment discussed way back in Chapter 1: it's not the work; *it's the way your deliver the work.*

Delivery is whatever you do to get your work in use *and* appreciated. Everyone has lost a good idea or had a smart proposition ignored. A good delivery technique is an all-important aspect of how you move the work along. While that depends on the quality of the work, the truth is, the more you want to take charge, the more your success will depend on the relationships you create along with the work.

People engage with you to build alliances, compete, give support or withdraw it, take offense, admire, or applaud. I don't think Edgar gave a hang about my sterling brand-building skills. He objected to my ignorance of the relationship the Bronfmans had with New York and the arts. He wasn't asking for my approval or any special services; he did think he should have my respect.

That's just one aspect of how different relationships at work are.

The Three Rs

Once the "three Rs" of school were called readin', 'ritin', and 'rithmetic. Today, I'd say our relationships at work call for the following three Rs:

Respect
Reputation
Recognition

You can offer all three to others, and you expect to be given all three of these as well. They will not simply be handed to you. These are your aims when considering relationships at work. They reflect the nature of work relationships, what you should ask of yourself as you engage with others and what you should offer. Failure to do so is exactly how women begin to cede leadership opportunities to men.

Respect

Respect should be your first response to the people you work with. The respect that operates at work is narrowly defined; it is respect for the specific qualities and unique capacities of every individual at the office. The way to engender a feeling of respect is to learn to be neutral and objective in your appraisal.

You may judge a personal friend with differing criteria: how often she calls, her realness in crisis, her empathy, and of course her loyalty and friendship. All of these must be placed secondary to offering respect to another in your work relationships.

> Respect is acknowledging that there's a whole amazing range of talents, approaches, responses, and qualities others have that may not be at all like yours.

In the ad agency, there were clients who always said they preferred the account executives who were most like them. I had to dissuade them of this opinion because new ideas and fresh thinking are rarely squeezed out of people who think alike, who are always in heated agreement. It's the unlike, the opposites, who cause something new to happen.

Sam had a relationship problem in her sophisticated digital company around the issue of respect. She had conquered the work, but she couldn't make it to the first R of relationships. Sam admitted in the workshop that she really didn't respect several people at her company, even her boss. Until everyone laughed at her surprising admission, she really hadn't thought about it.

Actually there were very good explanations for her way of judging others. Her brainy family's message was "We are all we need." A family of professors, they revered high achievement. They were not snobs, but great accomplishments inspired them. All Sam's siblings hit the top of the charts in school performance, as did Sam. This elite clan mentality was ramped up by Sam's own bred-in-the-bone trait: "I live in my own head. I'm most comfortable in my own thoughts. I prefer to observe."

Applying and interpreting the complexities of digital solutions were a breeze for Sam. Her coworkers said they could almost see smoke coming out of her office when she was on a project.

Sam and her management seemed to agree; she's perfect where she is, an expert and greatly valued as such. Perhaps no further relationship building is needed. Her boss (the one she thinks doesn't "get it") is probably saying, "I don't care how she does it, so long as she does it." This was our conclusion until Sam dropped the other shoe—her "before" portrait:

BEFORE SELF-PORTRAIT

I AM A BRAIN IN A JAR.

She didn't draw a jar, but her words were plenty visual. Sam felt encased in a transparent prison; she could see out but was not fully engaged with others. Brain on, relationships off. No one who likes her situation carries a self-image like that.

She knew how esteemed her brain was. There was a centrifugal force acting to keep her in the jar—her own inclinations, the messages from the clan, and her management. What could get her out of that jar? Only a strong desire: she added to life in a jar, "I am missing out on too much."

Understated but intense—a good description of Sam. Her into-the-future portrait is the same set of words with a small addition:

AFTER SELF-PORTRAIT

I AM A BRAIN IN A JAR . . . WITH FEET.

When we asked what the feet represented, Sam replied hesitantly, "Those are all the relationships I will enter, I hope. I don't think I can change the brain in a jar, but I can offer to travel around more, investigate the qualities of others." She has decided to learn what her boss excels in and find ground on which they can meet in mutual respect.

Sam wants some respect too for who she is beyond her digital brain. She's afire with ideas for new applications for their company and even how to manage their ragged relationship with a dominant client. "It's so obvious to me, like the world is round, but they don't think I'm good at this stuff." Respect is a two-way street; the entry point is respecting how differently others may view a situation. You are offering to build a relationship by respecting who they are and understanding what it is they offer.

Reputation

Reputation is the glue that holds relationships together. It's an outward assessment of who is in there. Does your reputation, the one you are creating every day, reflect your self-portrait? Reputation is not something you are assigned at work; you learn to build it deliberately. If you're serious about communicating who you are, you have pulled out of your portrait the qualities you want to be known for.

> Building a reputation for your own qualities supersedes all other forms of engaging.

It's not being calculating like hiring a press agent, though that's a legitimate option. It's being careful to always communicate your highest potential. You will learn to be alert to misunderstandings (yes, I did want to be included in that meeting), diminishment (I'm not hesitating; I am thoughtful), and vigilant for every chance to present how you want to be known. To change the before portrait view of you they're holding, you may need to be aggressive about engaging in reputation-changing actions or words.

From Mother Hen to Eagle

Katherine originally called herself a "mother hen," with a before picture of chicks clustered around a fat brown hen. In the womanly virtues, Katherine ranked herself as very nurturing, collaborative, empathetic, peacemaking, modest, selfless, and dutiful. She defended these traits because they formed a core part of her family influences. She came from a matriarchal family. Her mother, plus the women cousins and aunts, made the decisions and took care of the whole extended family. When a cousin fell on hard times, Katherine's mother pulled everyone together to make the mortgage payments until the cousin could recover.

At this point, Katherine's reputation came directly out of that family orientation: "I am a team unifier, a leader by consensus rather than fiat. Although I tackle issues with a dogged tenacity, I really don't like disharmony. I think this makes me compromise on some important issues."

She began to question the mothering role she takes to so naturally. "I need to be less of a mom. I'm not sure people are looking for moms at the office."

Then a reality check hit: "The best of my chicks don't need to be babied anyway. They're the real raptors." She resolved to move from mother hen to motivator, replacing the hen in her portrait with a soaring eagle, still nested but able to fly up and away too. Katherine may know she's an eagle in the making, but her company has been trained to rely on "Mom."

Now that Katherine was able to feel the frustration of being tagged caring instead of able to soar on her own, she was alert when her chance came. Her general managers were discussing a job opening for a design department head. They were clearly not thinking of Katherine; in fact, not even looking at her. She was sitting on the side. As they talked, she leaned forward and actually raised her hand. "I'll take it," she said.

First they were astonished, then said they'd get back to her. One week later, they gave her the job. Her bold gesture suggested to them a more daring Katherine than they had seen before. "Katherine," her boss confided to her, "we always suspected you had this kind of courage; we were glad to see it emerge."

Katherine's own personal trait, which she called "covert bravery," rose up and out to be heard. In that one key moment, Katherine raised her hand and asked for the challenge.

You have a covert kind of bravery of your own. It's asking at the right time and the right place, and it helps secure your reputation for taking the initiative.

Herminia Ibárra tracks the work scene for women in her various studies. I met Herminia as the striking Harvard professor who showed up at Ogilvy to do a case study on leadership. An article she wrote, "Why Men Still Get More Promotions Than Woman," published in the *Harvard Business Review*, was all about the lack of reputation that haunts women at work: women are simply not chosen or seen as leaders. They do

> Don't follow your natural inclination and wait to have your reputation catch up with you; take charge of this part of the relationship yourself.

not have a reputation for being leaders in the eyes of the "deciders." She reports that big companies, desperate to get their women known and considered, not only give them mentors but have upped the ante by assigning them sponsors who are held responsible for helping get the women to the next level. This can backfire when a woman is promoted and then dumped by the sponsor, leaving her isolated and undefended in a new position. The study also mentions that women are learning to navigate the fine line between "being controlling" or "lacking presence" as leaders—issues around our reputation and our relationships and whether we can lead . . . like a man.

The curious thing is, you'd be willing to help others advance their reputation by speaking for them; why not for yourself?

> Learning to navigate; get a positive reputation based on your inherent qualities, presented by you with clarity and confidence.

Recognition

Recognition is your media plan for getting the word out on what you want to be known for and to everyone you think needs to know. An astonishing number of the women I've met in workshops are not known to their own bosses or top clients. In my career there were so few women that I stood out, maybe for all the wrong reasons. But I rarely had to introduce myself. The benefits of being recognized, by name alone or, better, by a reputation deep and wide, are immense.

When I cold-called those possibly irate Ogilvy clients in my first months as CEO, my name and a few aspects of my reputation were known. Not a single CEO refused or balked at my request for a private meeting. They had heard of me and were curious. That access was priceless in allowing me to speak honestly to them about Ogilvy.

But I've also learned from my women's classes that it's not easy to stand out. A surprising number reported they knew people who hired a public relations company to get the word out. Honestly, I think you are your own best ambassador, but you need to develop a personal media plan.

Remember to develop relationships with "influencers," which certainly includes other departments and people who work with you. They will move up with impressions of you that they pass on. Also, it's shortsighted and disrespectful to ignore adjacent departments and lower-level people.

Since Sam's ultimate "brain in a jar" portrait was given feet to travel, her first adventure out of the jar was to be known for being more than a digital genius, although she knew that her narrow but deep expertise was what her management wanted of her. She chose an interesting but indirect path to changing her reputation with management. She began writing think pieces for the industry's special interest magazines about the broader issues of when and how to use digital and even produced a guide on digital software. These subjects had been hidden in Sam's brain for years. When these essays were eagerly accepted by the magazines, approved first by her clients, she made sure her general managers saw them, even quoting one of them in the articles. Shameless.

It was quite a way to launch a new reputation. Her clients invited her to participate on panels. Her management asked her to be on the orientation team for new hires. She didn't have to ask or make a cold call, which for Sam would have been agony. But she did present her thinking; only this time, she picked a larger, more open-minded channel to send it through to her bosses. Part of gaining recognition is to manage "up" where the oxygen thins.

> Your primary relationship vector is up.

Managing up is scary. But only communicating down to juniors or sideways to your peers is not good enough. Steady yourself. You can only honor the promise of your self-vision if you learn to deliberately manage up.

The men (and occasionally women) who have the power to evaluate and promote you are often at a distance, whether on a different floor or in a different city. They may seem to be a remote and unknowable audience. Even so, you must build recognition at all levels. No one who sits over you will dig deep enough or watch you closely enough to accurately assess your potential or even get to know you. You may not know the outer limits of your ambition, but you know more than they do and it's your job to present that.

Joanna, who attended my seminar in Brussels, did not want to even call her boss in the United States. "He walked right past my door when he was here last, and he cut off my last presentation. I don't think he likes me."

"Hello! Joanna! It's not personal. It could be a thousand other things. So call," I insisted.

After she screwed up her courage and asked for a meeting with the boss, she reported, "He was clearly glad to hear from me, and we had a great meeting. He's got the world on his shoulders." She got a passing glance at his portrait: he's in a struggle to stay on top of a new job. You can confirm that you're headed in the right direction (up) if you're nervous before the meeting.

As one of six undersecretaries at the massive State Department, I felt Colin Powell's power (and reputation) as secretary of state looming over me. I still had to learn to shape my own reputation at State and apply for recognition; to take myself to that vast corner office of his, hushed and forbidding, with two clearance checkpoints and security guards watching me carefully. I didn't go often enough, leaving the secretary of state out of the loop on our more controversial projects. I had an excuse you'll recognize: "I didn't want to intrude on his many major world issues." It wasn't my recognition that suffered. It was appreciation and support for some of our programs.

Even as CEO at Ogilvy, I needed to be better known to Martin Sorrell, the head of our parent holding company. I asked to speak to *his* board about brand stewardship and not about profits, always their main focus. It was pretty awful. An erudite banker fell sound asleep, and we could all hear him snuffling. But you'll learn to just plow on as I did, because these efforts have residual power. Another member of the WPP board that day was a Harvard professor, and he passed along a recommendation to the Harvard grad school. "Keep an eye on Ogilvy. There's something interesting going on." Out of that came the Harvard case on Ogilvy as a successful turnaround. Very impressive to our clients.

> Of course, reputation and recognition together create the ultimate effect, especially in the upper halls of management.

Ironically, even a mediocre reputation that's widely known is better than "Who?" because an inadequate reputation can always be represented with no time diverted to being introduced. That's what most well-known products go through during their brand cycle—a constant series of reintroductions.

RALEIGH RE-PRESENTS

There's some truth to the Hollywood maxim that there's no such thing as bad publicity. I learned a lot from Raleigh, a young woman who acted in exactly the wrong way to gain a reputation. But her brand awareness, the reputation she created, was so powerful it eventually helped her move through a big organization. She was in-famous before she was famous, at least in her company. But her notoriety actually helped speed along a much needed change in her reputation.

When I was CEO of Tatham, at dinner with three department heads at Procter & Gamble, I was excited at the prospect of getting a new assignment. Unfortunately, it was my female wisdom they were seeking, not a brand contract.

Women were being cultivated in many areas at P&G, but Raleigh had them stumped. It took these sophisticated men about twenty minutes to finally reveal the true nature of their problem with Raleigh: she dressed provocatively, deliberately so, they felt. She wore very short skirts and no hose, but the kicker was, they told me with red faces, she also wore see-through blouses with no bra. It was a no-bra era in the agency too, but no one wore any-thing as transparent as Raleigh, or flaunted it quite so boldly. I stopped being amused by their discomfort when they asked me to talk to her.

The next week, Raleigh came to our agency very much in form, wearing a thin sweater, no bra, and a skirt with a deep slit. She hesitated when I motioned her into my office; I think she knew what was coming. A fierce advocate for women, I was also known to be demanding. I gave her a big hug and, still smiling, asked the burning question. "So, Raleigh my dear, what do you want to be known for, your breasts or your brain?"

*She was taken aback, but then she smiled and told me that her
wardrobe was her protest against the "no mavericks" culture at
P&G. I admired her for battling that conservative model, but her
racy reputation was not helping show her real qualities—being inventive and having a wealth of ideas—to be recognized.*

*I suggested she draw on this verve and daring to apply for an
international post. She took my advice and was soon sent to Italy,
where all the women looked as sexy as she did, and there she broke
new ground for P&G brands. She became a big player. Finally, a
U.S. health care company stole her away to be their CEO. They
wanted her because she was now known to be a person who could
survive in the trenches and was unafraid to innovate. Not a bad
reputation.*

Ironically, Raleigh was known throughout P&G (in an infamous
way I grant you) before she pulled her big turnaround, but that recognition ended up helping her develop a new and improved reputation. So
please keep your bra on while you deliberate about how to be known far
and wide for your unique qualities—but don't leave these deliberations
to others.

What Goes Around, Comes Around

Reputations ebb and flow. If yours is at low tide, keep your eyes on the
horizon. Many a brand has been resurrected from the depths or given
new life through an improved reputation and wide recognition.

When I resigned from J. Walter Thompson to join Tatham, I was
wounded because people didn't even say good-bye, much less arrange
a farewell lunch. Burt Manning, then creative director, did stop by.
Always astute about how people behave, he let me have it. "You've
played a big role here. Now everyone has to explain to clients and to
themselves that your leaving does not matter," he said. He made his
point by swinging his arm in a wide downward arc. "Even as we speak,
your reputation is diminishing."

When your reputation is on a fade, it's good to recall what my friend Joe said: "Remember, it's a long life." Neither Burt nor I knew then we'd both have a turn at being chairman of J. Walter Thompson, the mighty university of advertising. Both of our reputations survived intact.

Men have learned to tread lightly at the office, making as few enemies as possible. It's really just good form. Men can compete ferociously with each other, and then turn around and lend a hand to their defeated opponent. There's a practical reason we women should emulate this: it's a small world, and almost everyone comes back around. Work is a circle. You will be amazed at how people keep turning up to affect your life at work. Every relationship can have a long life.

> Almost every boss I've ever had ended up reporting to me, which is not a bad perspective to have as you contemplate your current boss.

When Bill Ross, my revered creative director, became head of the JWT Chicago office, I reported to him. Then he went on to international responsibilities as I began my stint at Tatham. After I became CEO and Tatham had turned the corner, I asked Bill to join us as our top creative guru. Now he reported to me. We could shift roles because wc had a deep mutual respect that left room for the relationship to circle back around.

When I returned to JWT years later as chairman, a fellow who had once been my supervisor now reported to me. Ten years before, he had gotten drunk at a client dinner and cut me down sarcastically. Now he appeared in my spacious office red-faced and sweating. He asked belligerently (subtlety was not his style), "Are you going to fire me?" That old history was still vivid to both of us. I pretended to think about it and then let him off the hook. "I'm your chairman, not your executioner."

He left as abruptly as he'd arrived, but I knew he felt uneasy. What goes around really does come around. My counsel to women who are angry and offended, especially by the way other women in authority behave, is to speak out but don't slash and burn. Also, you don't want to fire someone brutally because you're embarrassed and uncomfortable and then have him turn up as your new customer. Remember, it's a circle. My mental motto was, Treat everyone as though you are named in their will.

Leadership Relationships

In study after study, men are thought to be more likely leaders than women. This is a common enough fiction that you need to think about how to combat it directly. It's an attitude issue first of all: your attitude. One thing you can do is enter any room or group or debate absolutely determined not to miss an invitation to lead.

Attitude Enhancers

- See yourself as a leader, quit yielding the field of leadership to the men . . . please!
- Learn to participate in relationships with the same fierce passion men use to get promoted and take over. They may dodge intimate dialogue, but they understand that they have to demonstrate passion to show they are capable of sustained, intense fervor on behalf of a project or goal.
- Men compete with a whole heart, so vow to find your own way of competing.

Women have been warned not to "go all emotional" or "get pushy," so we tamp down these highly effective aspects of our relationships, preferring to keep ourselves as tailored as our trim black suits. It feels safer, and we fear being ostracized if we erupt in challenging situations.

But deep involvement and overt commitment to work is part of the passion that makes men so effective. As women, we are caught in a double bind. Sometimes we are fierce and fired up enough to take the lead, but other times we fall back and take things personally, withdrawing from a challenge or offended by the terms of the game. Is our tendency to take things personally part of the same passion that men use so effectively, or is it a handicap for women in the workplace? It's both.

Our problem is that taking things personally is how we read people. It helps us be more creative, in tune. I felt protective of this quality in women when Ralph, our creative director, came roaring into my office, waving his muscular arms like a windmill, exclaiming, "These women! They drive me crazy. They take everything so personally. I spend all my time apologizing, explaining, rephrasing. They see all of it as personal."

Ralph completely ignored my gender; he expected me to fix his problem with the women. I slowed him down, "Yes, Ralph. That's our gift." He looked exasperated, but I went on. "We see how people feel, and hear their subterranean messages. We are not afraid of intimacy (as you are). The fact that we're so sensitive explains why you have a creative team that's 90 percent female and why the work is so good."

I didn't give Ralph an inch. Nevertheless, when I saw an executive woman in our office react to a valid critique as a personal slight, I knew she was taking it too personally. Now she has a different problem. This will be the last honest appraisal she ever gets from her male coworker. Woman can view a blunt command as insulting (talking down to me) or changes in assignments as threatening (what does it mean?). This is when taking things personally slides down the continuum from "gift" to "not being professional" to "a pain to deal with."

> How others react when you take the lead isn't personal, it's work.

Men often see work as just another game, although they can be crushed by feeling like a zero unless they win big. We women are not always measuring whether there's a win in it for us. It's in our nature to weigh other aspects as well. Thus we have a reputation for being more resilient and adaptable, qualities that are evolving into esteemed assets for leaders.

Like men, we need to know how and when to display our positive passion at work. I have known men who are stiff as boards and never emote. But they don't get to be in charge. Now that you are as clear on your premier qualities as the men around you, the rest of the relationship puzzle is the ability to inspire and persuade others. These are the delivery qualities that make leaders and managers.

The top people want you to be passionate, fierce, and excited, but all in the name of bringing an idea or a group to the table and to completion. You'll notice friendship, or even loyalty or popularity, is not named as the important interaction between workers. They are benefits, but they don't replace the passion you are prepared to show on behalf of a good idea or substitute for the nerve to reject a bad idea. When you feel so strongly that you are prepared to be made vulnerable, that's a moment when you're in leadership. That moment has to come from your strength of conviction or zest for the task, not from some misplaced longing for love or approval.

> There is nothing as persuasive as a woman who cares fiercely about the issue at hand and is not afraid to let others know.

You and your portrait—your belief in yourself, your people, and your work—will one day be called on to make a stand, to take the lead.

When I was the undersecretary of public diplomacy at State, I was seated across the desk from Deputy Secretary Richard Armitage. He was clearly unhappy. Armitage doesn't speak, he growls, and he bench-presses some three hundred pounds, so his shoulders are almost as wide as his desk. He's intimidating to say the least. Also in the room was Lynne Cheney, who had been sent by the Near East bureau to kill or delay the program I was presenting to Armitage—two-minute documentaries on Muslim life in America that were slated to run on TV stations in Egypt, Indonesia, and other Muslim countries.

Armitage was uncomfortable because the bureaus (our state diplomatic core) were getting a lot of flak from the governments in those countries about my aggressive plan to take messages directly to their people. He said to me, after Lynne emphasized the harm the program could do (a complete reversal on her part, which I hadn't expected), "Beers, you should probably delay this effort." I completely lost my cool and my voice shook. "No. There will be no delay. This is the only program that has a chance to reach moderate Muslims. We have to have more of a dialogue than bombs and bullets."

He gave me an angry look, a look that has daunted three-star generals. And Lynne actually stood up to add her protest against my position. I didn't care. I looked only at Armitage. "This is what I came here to do," I said. That let him know that I'd take the conflict to Powell, to the president, to the heavens. At that moment I was very vulnerable in my fear that they'd wipe out a year's work by greatly talented people, and I was furious at this last-minute delay to kill the program.

We ended up running the program but with little support from the bureaus, which made it much less effective. But I'd take the same stand all over again. My pulse races even in the retelling. This was about betrayal, religion, war, power brokers, but it was also my moment to say no, to stand.

Ask Yourself These Questions

- Are men any more strategically sophisticated or decisive or committed to an idea than you are? No, they're just more willing to show it, more willing to put their beliefs on the line.
- Are men more capable of leading, inspiring, and persuading others than you are? No, but you have to add to your fine ability to understand and empathize with others, a willingness to commit to an unproven idea and take heat for supporting that idea.

R>W: When Relationships Matter Most

There comes a time when work shifts from being about the content of the meeting to your relationship with those in the meeting. This may happen during a meeting or in a phone call, or even in a tense barrage of emails. Because I was trained as a mathematician, I think of it like this: R>W. It's a moment when the relationship (R) is greater than (>) the work (W). You might want to tattoo this on your wrist as a reminder, because this shift is the point where many of us will tend to walk away to avoid being put in such an uncomfortable personal inter-action.

The moment you are put in charge of a new project or introduced to a different department or a whole new company, you should be ready for R>W. A new school principal longs for the old days when she was a teacher, and doctors who become department heads never give up all of their patients because there's more clarity to be found in mastering the work itself. You can actually do the work, stay on strategy, and enjoy the satisfaction that comes with conquering specific tasks—that's (W). It's easier than dealing with competitive relationships, the indifferent fence-sitter, the second-guesser, the bully, the troublemaker, even the loyal fan—that's (R).

A person who can rise to the challenging tasks of inspiring, motivating, and persuading others to act is already leading. Presenting your more fully formed portrait to others is not a matter of holding a business meeting, then creating a separate portrait meeting. If you don't do the one along with the other, guess which one you'll never get around to? I used to plead with the creative department to "build the brand as you demonstrate the product": I wanted to do both in the same thirty-second TV spot and so do you, to do the work and build the relationship at the same time.

> Here's the bottom line: the person who is very good at relationships is the one who gets to be in charge.

When we talked about the features of the American Express card (the work), we also needed to remind people it was more than a card; it was a safety net (the relationship). By ending the message with the line, "Don't leave home without it," we were reminding users of their relationship with the card.

I once led a workshop of women who were considered ready to move into more demanding levels of management. Though they came from different industries—management consulting, packaged goods, and university development (fund-raising)—they were all about to enter into a new set of relationships at work. I could glimpse the nature of these relationships in very specific appraisals from their management that arrived along with the women. In addition to high praise about their brain power and capacity to do the work well, their sponsors wanted them to be ready for a change in how they delivered the work; to learn to lead.

Their managers talk about leadership in these words:

> "She needs a more expansive view of leadership. Going from on-line to corporate means people see her differently. Now when she says, 'This is the plan,' they need to sign on, to follow her and the plan."
>
> "In leading an all male sales group, Lydia has to know how to fit in and not get bluffed by their tough guy antics."
>
> "The truth is Sabrina is not a people person, but she's too talented to be left behind. She needs to learn to mix in the emotional with the rational. Also, I'd like to see her have more presence."

The message is clear: you will express your leadership in such moments when the relationship prevails.

TRANSFORMING A RELATIONSHIP

Lydia was the "ice maiden." She knew that she was inadequate in her relationships in her new position as a Sales Department manager. Her before portrait, an ice sculpture isolated in splendor on a banquet table, had been transformed into an after portrait with this promise: "Let me tell you my story," delivered with arms open wide. The contrast between her after and before portraits was a war between the safety of the work and an impassioned delivery of herself and the work. Lydia was deeply influenced by the idea that you should "never let them see you sweat," a message from her father. Her mother's message froze her up too. "Don't care so much; it'll only make you unhappy."

She reacted by immersing herself in her work as if she were lost in another world. That intense focus got her promoted, but now that she was a sales manager, she knew she had to learn how to create relationships with the boys' club, her new peer class.

Her "consumer research" was no help. "It wasn't negative; it is just that they don't get me. I guess that's not too surprising—I haven't let anyone know me." She knew she'd never lead anyone without being willing to reveal some heart, to be vulnerable, to risk being known. She decided to try to introduce her new, more open way to the other four sales managers, to "tell her story." "They couldn't think more highly of themselves; it's like they have a private club," she said to me.

"On the other hand," I reminded her, "it's hard to cuddle up to an ice maiden. Let them know you."

Not sure how, Lydia suddenly remembered a raunchy sales film from one of her clients. He had been moved to tears of laughter as he played it for her. It was outrageously funny but crude; not her style.

She invited the other sales managers to a 6:00 PM session. The guys were very curious about a meeting called after hours, but leery. She started by saying that since they were all partners, sharing in a department-wide quota, she wanted to share a new way to generate sales leads. Since this was work, she handled this part brilliantly. She could see they were impressed, but maybe feeling a little talked down to. Then she put in the DVD of the sales film and announced, "I brought you a present." They were frankly astounded that Lydia, of all people, was sponsoring the rowdy piece as it played out. The more they registered how quiet she was, the more they guffawed at the film's antics. At the end, they asked, "Lydia, this from you?"

And now she could smile as she confessed, "I hate this film." That set off more peals of laughter. "But I knew you'd love it," she said.

That clicked for her audience; she was willing to overcome her own distaste for such a gimmick because she liked and understood her audience well enough to know they'd get a kick out of it. Lydia was stepping out, willing to be vulnerable and asking to be included. Her colleagues never forgot how open she was that evening and, more surprising to them, how much fun. Overnight, her reputation was enhanced, her level of recognition wider, as the night of the sales film tale spread.

In a way, Lydia had it easier than most of us. She was a newcomer to the department, working with a relatively clean slate. I say "relatively" because the team had already collected the usual mishmash of fact and rumor, but her new storytelling, easygoing self was first up at bat with the boys' club.

It's harder to rewire existing relationships. Since your goal is to present your portrait every day along with your work, you need to learn to let the power of who you are get at least equal billing with the work that you do. That's what the critiquers mean when they say, "She needs more presence."

Presence, that magic silver bullet, is getting the relationship right and then learning to perfect your communication skills.

7

COMMUNICATION

I Hear You

ALLEN BROKE THE golden rule of communication: "It's not what you say; it's what they hear." His audience did not hear what he intended to communicate. He made this mistake in a very public arena as a headliner in a new business pitch. This mishearing was so serious, it cost him his job.

Allen, head of a creative group at J. Walter Thompson and famous for his one-liners, was wickedly funny but rather cruel. He was known as a forceful presenter, with a big voice booming out of his prizefighter's body. Allen had a thwarted craving for a career in comedy. His self-portrait was probably titled in his mind "The Great Entertainer."

Allen was chosen to be the key presenter at our first meeting with Kellogg's cereal division. Led by Sanders, their new division head, they had agreed to give the Thompson agency a first-ever review. Allen's role was to explain how easy it is for your message to get lost or misunderstood among all the other advertising messages in the marketplace. Such messages can be so poorly constructed they can mislead or confuse the audience. Much to our surprise, Allen then gave his own live demonstration of how a misleading message works: "If I say to you, 'I'm a tough character, virile and manly,' but then I *show*

159

you . . . " and he began to parody a gay man, bending his wrist delicately as he pranced his big bulk across the stage.

He stopped and turned, clearly expecting us to laugh, but we were all stunned into silence by his tasteless bit of theater. None of us knew then that Sanders, the much admired and respected division head, had recently told his Kellogg team that he was gay.

Allen was focused on showcasing his devastating wit. All he thought about was what he wanted to say. What he actually communicated was how oblivious he was to his audience. Even without the presence of Sanders, Allen was not communicating effectively to any of us.

Can You Hear Me?

Communicating is not just telling or showing. Sometimes you can emote, gesture, and implore but still fail to be heard. Here is an absolute truth about communication that no one can ignore or alter.

It's Not What You Say, It's What They Hear

Not being heard or being misheard is common—in politics, at work, in love, certainly in advertising. Every parent learns to say to a child, "Did you *hear* what I said?" Well, it's a good question.

If you can turn your focus away from what you want to say and toward what your listener can hear, you are on the way to becoming a better communicator. It causes a shift in your orientation that is as dramatic as the Golden Rule: "Do unto others as you would have them do unto you."

This rule, appearing in some form in every religion, asks us to stop and consider what might be heard or felt or experienced by another when we behave in a certain way. Our version of the Golden Rule exhorts us to stop and ask, "How will this be heard?"

It's not what you say, it's what they hear.

This rule pulls you away from the thoughts tumbling around in your brain about what to say and toward a focus on your listener. Of course, you are certain that *you* would never be as obtuse, as self-centered, as gross as Allen. But I warn you, you too will blunder if you are concentrating only on your own actions or words. To communicate effectively, you need to become adept at these two things:

Part I: Response: Calculate the *response* you're likely to receive.
Part II: Message: Resolve exactly *what* you want to say.

Don't try to get to the second discipline without first wrestling the first one, the likely response, to the ground.

Part 1: Assessing Their Response

Creating a desired response is not an accident, it's a discipline. When things are going well at work, you automatically anticipate your partner's responses, make a few mental adjustments, and then begin to say your piece. It's part of the natural rhythm you have with your team and your frequent contacts. If it's about the work we speak confidently knowing our thoughts will be received pretty much as intended. Facts, data, charts, and work exchanges are nice that way; they travel uninterrupted from speaker to listener. They can lull you into thinking you are a good communicator.

> Being able to relate the routine, logical, linear material only proves you are a good teller.

Your audience's response is, "I heard you say this." This is only the first step to truly communicating.

My first tutorial on the basic discipline of communicating came from a pair of "professors" at J. Walter Thompson: our creative star, Jerome Bullmore, out of London, and the man who invented the role of planner, Stephen King. They hammered into us the necessity of putting the listener's anticipated response into our communication plan well *before* we began to write ads. Of course, we would forget that, swept up into the magic of the product and diverted by the many different viewpoints around the table.

That's how I, a bright young account supervisor on Sears, made an electric chainsaw commercial that scared the intended listener right out of buying one. Our "intendeds" were first-time chainsaw users. We were so dazzled by the ability of this chainsaw to automatically sharpen the blade (!) that the demonstration of the sharpening became the whole TV spot. The poor greenhorns didn't even know chainsaws *needed* sharpening and were quite alarmed to hear it. We had failed to check in with our prospective buyers about their level of knowledge about a chainsaw. Their likely responses never made it into the communication plan.

Ask yourself at the very beginning: What is the response I want . . . or can hope for . . . or might expect? When your message is polished, your words at the tip of the tongue, consider again the likely response.

One of the most accomplished disciples of our JWT professors was Burt Manning, who, by keeping the client's response in mind, altered the outcome of a crucial presentation for Ken L Ration dog food. We were late getting to this important meeting, and Ken Mason, head of Quaker Foods, was frowning at us all. Burt began his presentation by wringing his hands and confessing what a huge problem this had been. He began to show the ads and ideas we'd all rejected, exposing all our stops and starts, our wrong turns.

"What *is* Burt doing?" we whispered. The clients were listening intently as step by step Burt went through the whole painful process, until at last, almost reluctantly, he presented the solution—which now seemed to be the one, the only solution.

The relief in the room was palpable. Our clients' acceptance of the solution came about because they had crawled backward through the missteps and slow discoveries, the messiness of the creative process that Burt revealed. They could see for themselves why this campaign was a winner.

Burt knew his listener, Ken Mason, well. He knew Ken would not have been in any of the earlier meetings, so he was a "cold" audience; he had to be brought up to speed. Further, he knew Ken would never trust a conclusion unless he thought rigorous steps had been taken to reach it. Burt never once lost sight of the response he wanted, rejecting the usual agency practice of a drum roll revealing one winning idea. Ken Mason's response, brief as always, was, "I think you've solved it."

A Love Letter to the Listener

To be properly heard, you need to anticipate your listener's response. The better you know your listener, his or her biases, orientation, and degree of subject knowledge, the more likely you are to deliver your message effectively.

You need a pretty good idea of what your listener thinks about the topic you're going to be covering—as well as how he feels about it.

Your listener's movie is always running and is full of biases, opinions, and odd reference points. The channel on which you're broadcasting is not clear and open and empty; it is full of earlier, possibly conflicting messages, beliefs, and experiences. It's a wonder anything ever gets through.

> Every listener will fit your message into the movie already playing in his or her head.

Just how much knowledge and understanding of your listeners you need to have in order to respectfully fit what you're saying into the movie of their life was dramatized to me like this: "You should know your listeners well enough to be able to write them a love letter." At least that's the ideal. In a potentially hostile encounter, you will find it even harder not to simply blurt out your feelings, say the wrong words. When it's going to be a difficult exchange, when you don't even like the listener, go back to your discipline. What can they hear? Anger, for example, can be a very effective communication tool, but not ungoverned, running from your mouth to their ears without gauging their likely response.

The less comfortable we feel around our listeners, the harder it is to remember to stop and try to anticipate their response.

It's ironic, but some of the smartest marketing women I know cannot remember a single communication discipline when they're confronting a relationship fraught with tension or unfair play.

TALKING PAST ONE ANOTHER

Diane wanted to change her new boss's negative evaluation of her. As soon as she heard that Grey had rated her "ineffective at leading her team," she began to rehearse her defense in a blaze of righteous anger. "I am proud of my ability to look out in front of our fast-moving client, Dell Computers. I know how to head off trouble."

Grey sees Diane's delivery as all gloom and doom. As he said, "She is forever telling us things are getting serious, the future has this problem, the sky is falling. Why does she do that? Her group is frightened, running scared, and demoralized. It's her only limitation, but it's a big one."

The two of them are talking right past each other. You'd think they were married. Diane could have learned more about Grey, their brand-new president. He felt he had a mandate to sell their digital division skills within a large traditional ad agency. He was thinking like a missionary, focused on the possibilities. He needed to avoid any show of weakness. Diane could have unearthed that his favorite saying was "Suspend doubt!" The last thing he could hear was how bad things could get.

Every word you say, the way you look, and your body language are all stimuli to which the listener responds. Diane could have remodeled her stimulus, erased her frown and urgent gestures, and changed her message: "You know, Dell is so innovative, they are inventing the next frontier. My job is just to keep us all up, even ahead." Then the response from Grey would have been: "Diane is on top of this for us, while I'm fighting for our fame in the corporate halls."

Your Stimulus, Their Response

"Stimulus" is a good word to keep in mind when you're trying to decide what to say to elicit a certain response. Thinking about the stimulus gets you past thinking about the words you want to say and into the habit of considering everything that's part of your presentation. Are you frowning, twisting a pencil, tapping your foot, or letting your voice get squeaky? All of the above? Do you need a visual, a pause, a joke? Is there anything more intimidating than someone talking to you while glancing repeatedly at his watch? That's a stimulus of both words and actions.

Lydia, the "ice maiden," did not rely only on words when she set a meeting with the boys' club. Rather, she let a slightly risqué sales film delight her audience. They responded, "Well, I guess we don't know Lydia after all. She has quite a sense of humor."

Think of preparing a stimulus, not just a barrage of words. To activate more involvement, reach for a deeper level of hearing that includes curiosity or belief, even doubt, perhaps a shift of opinion. You might try an unusual simile as Jacques did.

Sex Is Stimulating

One evening in Chicago, I introduced our four partners in our newly merged agency, Tatham and RSCG (a European network), to a dazzling black tie audience of Chicago's business, social, and political elite at the beautiful Casino Club. Jacques Segula, called the Pope of Advertising in France, had the mike. We all strained to understand Jacques's Franco-English. He was describing how to save big new ideas, when he said something that sounded like "Eet iss lak a spern too say oh."

As the room burst into laughter, I realized he had just said, "A new idea is like a spermatozoa," a pretty graphic simile for a business dinner. I'd never thought of the wayward travels of the sperm to the ovum as being like the journey a new idea must take, but that night, Jacques made it impossible to forget.

To gauge a likely response you need to know as much as possible about your receiver. When I blew it with Edgar Bronfman Jr., my Seagram's client at the Whitney Museum event, I could have asked for a ten-inch thick dossier on Edgar and his father, who was being honored, which would have helped me understand my listeners. I didn't ask.

Remember, the best communication is unselfish. It's not telling; it's also listening and learning.

Walk in Their Shoes

Mary Baglivo is now a top executive at Saatchi Advertising. Even when she was a young woman at Tatham, she knew instinctively how vital it was to "walk in their shoes." She had a big job running our new brand, Old Spice Aftershave, but she couldn't get the P&G clients to approve any of the new advertising ideas. This recent acquisition was a very popular brand with the Procter & Gamble crowd; it was a lot more fun than all those laundry detergents the Procter men had trained on. The trouble is, they had strong and wrong ideas of what the ads should feature, like romance and wedding bells. Mary and her team discovered that their eighteen-year-old male users' views of women, romance, commitment, and even their vocabulary was light-years away from that of the slightly older men at P&G.

At an impasse, Mary created an unusual stimulus: a room where everything an eighteen-year-old male treasured was on display. The music, books, magazines, clothes, posters, even tapes of conversations, made it painfully clear that young men saw commitment as a loose kind of partnership, certainly nothing resembling marriage. The Old Spice client team was bewildered by the awful music, the magazines, the weird cartoons, the repulsive humor. They realized through this forced march into the "shoes of the eighteen-year-old" they were meeting an entirely different species of male. That recognition was the perfect response, and it got the new ads approved with not a single wedding bell in sight.

Part 2: What You Want to Say

Armed with insights and knowledge about what your audience may be able to hear, you can now decide what you want to say. This is the time to be precise, to hone in on the right words, the tone, the manner, the environment.

Find the Crux

First you need to identify your central idea—the crux—and ruthlessly eliminate anything that is tacked on, fussy, irrelevant. Part of the discipline in determining what to say is to say less, not more.

This discipline to eliminate the extraneous will make you a more effective communicator. You will be heard, and heard loud and true. It's the opposite of "spilling." This is a term I heard repeated from members of AA meetings to describe someone who just lets everything spill out in the meeting, with no editing for clarity or relevance, just a barrage of emotions and random tales and unconnected pieces.

Women have a tendency to spill. It's that verbal agility of ours that we can overrely on. Especially when we're nervous or uneasy, out comes a torrent of words. When this happens the listener is free to pick out what's important and then we wonder, "Where did he get that idea?"

When you choose a central thought from a lot of other options, you are making it easier for others to understand you. If people often miss your point, that's probably because you

> The one who is holding a clear picture of the crux issue, well defined and smartly tailored down to its tightest form, will be the one who is in charge of the conversation.

did not have the discipline to eliminate every irrelevant word, expression, or idea. Communicating well is a competitive advantage.

I had one early, fleeting experience with the potency of getting to the crux when I was a new account executive at JWT. It took me some years to become much more deliberate about choosing the right thing to say, but this time, I did get right to the crux.

I was living my fairly meek life as the first female account executive on the Alberto Culver account when, passing a conference room, I heard the distinctive voice of Marion Howington. Marion was the only executive woman at the agency and she was formidable. Already a creative director, she was known for her sharp tongue and even sharper brain. To me, she seemed to have it all: family, social position, command of her work, and respect from all fronts. That's why it was all the more crushing when I realized that Marion was doing a dead-on mockery of me and my Texas drawl, to the obvious delight of the men in the room. "Aym not sure it's the rahyt thin to do" is what I heard. I recognized myself immediately. The men laughed . . . and laughed some more. Alone in the hall, I felt the heat rise in my face and a lump form in my throat.

For days I walked around too self-conscious to speak much. I had to get beyond this humiliating episode, and I kept running endless tapes of what I might say to Marion. I could be angry, pleading, demanding, anything to restore my confidence. When I finally walked into Marion's fancy office, she didn't bother to look up until I shut the door, which caused her to raise her head in surprise. I was so relieved to finally get this over with that I spoke in a clear and firm voice, not at all drawly. "I'm not leaving here until you and I, the only two professional women in this place, can agree to present a united front to the men. They are greatly amused at our willingness to diminish each other."

I just stood there. She smiled slightly and then shrugged on her perfectly tailored red jacket and asked, "What are you doing for lunch?" Marion became my ally and friend for life. There was a very interesting reaction around the office: the men developed an elaborate caution around us. We were only two, but now it was two-squared.

I did not know enough then to anticipate Marion's response (a terrifying thought), and I didn't have a communication plan. But even in my personal anguish and dread of the moment, I got to the crux of the issue. If we couldn't unite as women, the men would really enjoy the show. I could have set it up more gracefully, rather than blurt it out, but I did instinctively add a strong stimulus to the import of my words . . . I shut the door.

A Crux System

Getting to the crux is another way to describe the strategic process that eliminates everything not relevant to or supportive of the core idea or mission. But first we have to identify the core idea. Many of the women in the workshops, justly admired for their strategic abilities at work tasks, are the same women who lose the ability to strip things down to the central issue when there is office drama, politics, or intensely competitive relationships to deal with.

Also when we are the ones with the strong emotional responses, we often find ourselves at a loss for words, or at least the right words. Just when we most need clarity, we are running defensive scenarios or anger tapes or reverting to childish patterns or "wifey" words. When relationships test your fortitude, walking away or withdrawing or stalling are not good options, either.

My crux system was adopted by the women, even the ace strategic thinkers, because when you're in a swirl of reactions, not sure what to say, the best thing to do is take it all apart. I learned this system in math class. When I felt overwhelmed by options, I learned to stop and separate out, piece by piece, everything I had jammed together into one messy quandary.

In my first year out of college, I taught engineering algebra to twenty-five men at night school in Texas. My earnest students must have felt alarmed to see how young their teacher was, dressed in loafers and socks. They were all five to ten years older than I, but this course was a crucial prerequisite for a degree in engineering. That engineering degree was the standard for how a good man earned his living in Houston, Texas. In our math class, there were word problems that were pages long. When I saw how serious the men were and how they depended on me, I had no choice but to stay up late every night to untangle those wretched word problems so I could translate them in a simpler way for my class. I learned to lay out every point and then reassemble all the unanswered issues around the one that seemed most key: the crux.

Almost without realizing it, I began to use this method at work to unravel issues I faced that were not as orderly or manageable as many business issues, ranging from big but unproven ideas to traumatic relationship problems. Here's the approach: pull it all apart. You start by laying out every single element that's tumbling around in your confusion about how to respond to a relationship problem. The trick here is not to link up the pieces that are cluttering up your mind. (You said this, so that means . . .) Each piece has to stand on its own so you can see its importance in a neutral, unconnected way.

SAYING TOO MUCH

I was working with Irene's company after she had returned to her textile design firm following a maternity leave. In her absence, an "empty suit," as she called him, began to sabotage her meetings, especially when they put on shows of their new designs to retailers. Bill was known to her retail buyers, but he didn't have anything to do with the design work and he was jealous of Irene's impact. Often he interrupted, saying, "Well, that's one look; there are others . . . "

"He is driving me crazy; he is making us look divided in our meetings. He has to be handled," she told me. I asked her to lay out every option she felt she had to deal with Bill.

"I can tell the general manager Bill is a problem."

"I can try to show him where he's wrong."

"I can ask him not to come to this next big meeting."

"I can tell him he's an ineffective jerk."

"Jerk" was what she wanted to say. She wanted to let him have it, but she felt it would only please him to know how he rattled her. When asked to find the crux, she said, "Well, I guess the big issue is that he's damaging our presentations and making us look like a divided team."

"I agree, so how could you say that?" I asked.

"I could say, 'You're hurting our new business efforts and you need to back me up,'" she concluded.

"Only the first half of that sentence speaks to the crux," I said, and I explained that the crux needs to be clear and simple, like this: "It's completely unacceptable for you to derail the content of our presentation." To then add "you need to back me up" asks him to do something he doesn't want to do and it isn't necessary anyway.

Irene had linked the key issue, Bill's sabotaging interruptions, with her feelings, "you need to back me up," and it weakened her main message.

My father used to tell me, "never explain, never complain." We overexplain or add on because we feel tense when we have to make a stand. But when we pile on other ideas, we weaken the ability of the receiver to hear or to believe that we mean what we say.

Let the Crux Rise Up and Out

Stare at your possible options until one emerges as the central issue. You can test to see if it is indeed the most important by removing it and seeing if the whole problem alters with that strand gone. The good news is because the crux is the central issue around which everything else circles, when you get to the crux, you're more than halfway to knowing what you want to convey. Getting to the crux is the same strategic process companies use to allocate resources. You are choosing among options, and all the options available to you are not equally good.

> Until you take every strand apart, you cannot see the worth of each item on its own.

Because it's jamming your brain, your problem is not going to yield to a resolution until you find its center. How you feel is usually not the crux, but you need to lay out those feelings so you can see them and then set them aside. Some issues or messages can now be discarded, for they don't affect the crux. Some ideas or reactions that once seemed central will now take on a different meaning.

THE RIGHT WAY

Maria, a lawyer, didn't agree with her partners that they should yield to their client's insistence on a faster and cheaper solution to what he saw as a lawsuit designed to harass him. "The problem is that his 'easy' way won't work in the long term," she insisted, coming to what she felt was the crux.

The upcoming meeting promised to be unpleasant. During the meeting her partners nodded uneasily as the client, in cowboy boots and denim shirt, slammed the notebook on the table to punctuate how he'd handle the lawsuit by his "attacker." Then he snapped at Maria because she wasn't nodding. "Well?"

"We can do it your way," she answered carefully, and then she waited a long beat, "or we can do it right."

He glared at her and then threw back his head, almost tipping his chair over in a burst of laughter. "I just wondered if you meant what you said about how to fix this" was his surprising response.

Earlier Marie had rehearsed in her mind what to say and how she was going to handle the client they called The Cowboy. She had anticipated his response. She wanted to be succinct and understated because this client didn't like challenges, but she felt that agreeing with him would be costly for him and the firm.

Reorder the Pieces

Now stack each issue in order of importance to the central point you've identified. This is what problem solvers do when they eliminate many options and find one good solution or "saying." This is a time to use your self-portrait. It's your guide to finding, among the one or two possible stimuli, the one that is truest to who you are, an appropriate message for you to deliver. Once the messy pieces are sorted out, the irrelevant points acknowledged and then laid aside, the crux has a chance to show up.

> When the crux is found, the remaining factors ranked in order of their importance to this central issue, what to say becomes obvious.

What to Say in a Mutiny

The most troublesome period at Ogilvy came when I faced a confrontation with a group who felt I wasn't cutting it as their CEO. Given all the emotions surrounding this issue, the ultimate crux turned out to be totally different from what my first reactions suggested.

At a low period early in my second year, I didn't have many admirers; my colleagues were in "watch and wait" mode. One of my more devoted team members did come to me with an urgent message: "There's a group of top people who are plotting to oust you!" He was alarmed. "There's still time, but you need to show them who's boss around here."

It was the worst possible news coming at a bad time. Though we had a strong first year, winning Jaguar and wooing back American Express and Ponds in what the press called Operation Win-Back, we knew we had to stir up more momentum worldwide. In view of our uncertain progress, I felt I could not lift my head to receive this new blow. Our conversation was interrupted by a client's arrival, and then I rushed to

Aspen for the only vacation I'd had all year, taking the menacing idea of the evil cabal (as I had named them) on the trip with me.

The next evening, I was having dinner at a posh café in Aspen with three good friends. Since I could think of nothing but the mutiny, I asked my dinner companions what they would do if a group were trying to unseat them. "I'd hire a detective to dig up dirt on them," said Angela.

"I'd fire the top two and demote the others," said Tom, her husband.

"I think I would bring them together and ask them why they didn't like me" was the approach from Memrie, a woman who was in fact so beloved by everyone in New York, she probably really wanted to know. We laughed at her "Ms. Popularity" approach.

It was fun to hear unlikely solutions, but I knew in every fiber of my being that I was on my own on this one.

I went off to what was a long, dark night in the Rockies. I had decided to turn to my old faithful technique for separating out emotional issues, but I was not sure it would work for something as dire as a mutiny. Crowding in for attention came all my resentments of this crew as well as anger and pain; it really hurts to have good people act against you. I had to admit that a few people had made it clear they didn't believe in our new vision of brand stewardship, or in me. Finally, I accepted that I wasn't likely to convert them. I was pushing for changes they didn't like.

Once I concluded that the mutiny really wasn't personal, I was able to lay aside my feelings of being personally attacked. I spent the next hours debating whether we had the organizing vision I hoped would give the creative, research, and media departments something to rally around. The merits of brand stewardship could only play out in the months to come, but it helped a lot when I said to myself, out loud in the dark, "Well, I don't have any better idea, and neither does anyone else. This is it."

Was this the crux, that we had this *one* big idea on which to bet the future? If so, should I summon the resources and the energy to defeat the growing mutiny?

That's when the true crux emerged. It was an energy issue all right; not to defeat the mutiny but to conserve my own energy for a larger purpose.

We were trying to change the way Ogilvy researched, advertised, and developed brand relationships. Such a change meant that we had to bring hundreds of offices into the loop and sell the idea to just as many clients. I would need every ounce of my time, energy, and persuasive skill to help accomplish this scale of change. That was the central issue: **I could not afford to divert my energy into trying to forestall a mutiny.**

If we succeeded in getting brand stewardship accepted by our clients and our own people, the cabal would be rendered powerless. If we didn't, I was cooked anyway. That was my new order of importance. I was now ready with what I wanted to say when I called back my worried confidant in New York. I interrupted him in midsentence. "Please do not tell me more. I don't even want to know who you think is involved. At this point, I have decided to do . . . nothing."

If I hadn't been able to take such a scary problem apart, in the process I've described, I might have wasted precious time and energy on my first reaction—trying to take on the mutiny directly. Instead, I put every ounce of energy I had into building a new Ogilvy and didn't lose a moment trying to defeat "old" Ogilvy.

Brand stewardship did help usher in a new era of prosperity for Ogilvy. Months later, our momentum assured, I gave the ringleader of the cabal, now known to me, a bland corporate title to buy him some time to look for a new job. I remember saying, "John, it's obvious you can't support our new direction, and this is where the whole agency is going. You need to go where you can be wholehearted about your work." That was the crux of that farewell message and exactly what I wanted to say to him, only more politely.

Our objective skills can disappear like smoke when we feel anxiety about confronting a personal injustice or holding up a hand to say "choose me." Culling out everything extraneous allows us to acknowledge swirling resentments, biases, and anger and then get them out of the way. The wordy, overexplaining, too grateful side of you is shelved, and you and your portrait know exactly how to say what you want to say; to evoke the very response you have in mind.

The crux process helps us sort through what to say when a relationship turns unfair or mean-spirited, or when we are seeking to make our potential known, or choosing just the right cues to illustrate an important aspect of who we are.

> When you have an estimate of the response you'll evoke and have nailed down the crux of an issue, then you will speak in a way that will be deeply heard.

The right message is not restricted to traveling logically through the brain, it also enters the heart of the listener. That's not to say it is romantic, but it is a pure expression of feeling backed up by will and conveys a different weight than the many purely factual messages that our brains receive day after day.

To say exactly what you mean and to have it heard on this deeper level is how work becomes more satisfying.

8

PRESENTATIONS
Informing, Asking, Confronting

TEDDY FORSTMAN DIDN'T actually know the golden rule of communication—It's not what you say, it's what they hear—but he proved to be a master of the concept and took it one step further. He got his messages heard well enough to create new demand for one of the world's most expensive and enviable luxuries, a private airplane.

Teddy and his company acquired Gulfstream Aeronautics, maker of the sleek private jets. Gulfstream had a new G-4 model coming to the market and a backlog of the earlier G-3s as well. It would only cost you about $35 million to take home a new Gulfstream.

As the new owner and acting CEO, Teddy had inherited a boatload of problems—make that a planeload—including too many planes in inventory, airports that didn't have long enough runways for the newer planes, and worst of all, Gulfstream's lackluster reputation prior to the acquisition. I was on Teddy's board, and when I say I was the small player on that board, I am not being modest. Also sitting around the table were Donald Rumsfeld, Michael Ovitz (the mega Hollywood kingmaker), Robert Strauss (counselor to four presidents), General Colin Powell, Roger Penske (of Penske Trucks), Henry Kissinger, George Shultz, and other such luminaries.

The Gulfstream management team briefed Teddy that the prospective buyers of a new G-4 already had huge departments that selected and maintained the company planes. It was these departments, they said, who were the deciders on new airplane buys, but Gulfstream was now having a hard time even getting in the door. There were other good planes available with new features for less money. Gulfstream, once the gold standard, often wasn't even in contention.

As the new G-4 was readied for sale, the G-3 refitted, and the many production problems solved, Teddy decided the crux of the problem Gulfstream faced was a need to get into the hallowed halls of the CEOs, and internationally to top clients such as various royal family buyers. If Gulfstream took the slower, predictable route through the purchasing departments, the reduction in the inventory of planes would come too late. He needed a new kind of sales force to do the presenting and the asking.

That's when his startled board heard about our new assignment: we were to be that sales force. We were to get the G-4 in contention through our wide range of contacts. This was no typical role for a private board, which is usually one of appraiser and counselor. Teddy felt we could present the Gulfstream directly to CEOs or wealthy prospective owners, all of whom might care more than their purchasing departments did about the differences in flying distance, the comfort, and the prestige the new Gulfstream offered. He was willing to upend the selling process, top to middle, instead of the usual way from middle to the top.

We were given lists of likely buyers to call. I had to learn everything about the wonders of the G-4. I had no trouble loving the product because it was a thrilling ride. A number of my fellow board members had their own "Gs." I had only rarely flown in one, which didn't do much for my self-assurance. Nevertheless, when I saw two CEOs from Proctor & Gamble and General Motors on the list, I had to admit I knew them both. I nervously picked up the phone and alerted them, "There's a Gulfstream G-4 coming to your neighborhood." To my immense relief, both companies bought G-4s: I earned my wings.

Teddy wasn't worried about the message or the product. He was searching for an exciting and persuasive messenger—someone who could "ask" with conviction, who could be heard and trusted by his rarified target market. His instincts about their likely responses were dead-on too. Executives loved talking about and getting involved in the purchase of one of these great airplanes.

Presenters Get Out in Front of the Work

Life at work is just one presentation after another. In every email, meeting, conference, speech, or document bearing your name, you are presenting who you are and what you have to offer. Of course, you can bungle an opportunity to be clearly seen by hiding behind the work, making sure the lights are low, the power points dense with colored arrows and facts. You will then be a disembodied voice reading the charts everyone in the audience can read for themselves anyway. The better the visuals and the bigger the truckload of data, the harder it is to present yourself as a vibrant messenger.

> You can get all the disciplines of good communication right, but fail to enliven your own role as the presenter.

The women in my workshops make mini-presentations so we can see how they perform in the front of a room. They are at ease; they are clear and succinct presenters, usually backed up with sophisticated visuals. Their information is interesting, well organized, and well conveyed. However, the portrait of the person who is sponsoring all this effort is not much in evidence.

I ask the other students, "Who do you see here?" Usually they admit they've learned very little about the presenter other than her exterior qualities: smart, focused, serious, fast, strategic, and so forth.

Exceptions stand out, such as when Terry told a story in her presentation about the way her daughter uses toothpaste (she stirs it into a glass of water and dips her toothbrush in it) to make a point about how poorly people follow package instructions. All of a sudden we saw a loving mother who could make fun of herself and her daughter.

A presentation can be a highly concentrated opportunity to present yourself. You'll never command a room if you hide behind a report format or submit to a rigid company protocol of how charts are to be organized, where the speaker stands, and other such rules.

After viewing the women's presentations, we came up with a battle cry—Get out in front of the work!—to remind women that the presenter *is* the message.

Informing Doesn't Have to Be Sterile

Even though the majority of messages you are asked to deliver are meant to inform, reach conclusions, and convey results, there's still an opportunity to put yourself in the center of the data. You can be:

The interpreter
The proposer
The one who infers
The concluder

In reviewing material for your audience, you can draw inferences, propose actions, interpret the numbers, and lay out the consequences. That can turn an informing presentation into a much more interesting and involving one that evokes in your audience a response beyond "I heard you say this." To go beyond informing you need to be more than a backdrop for power points.

Think back to presentations you've made recently. How many times did you say, "I think," or "I believe"? Consider how the use of "I" quickens interest compared to the use of the neutral third person: "the report indicates," "it is established."

> Notice how much more arresting "I believe" is, than "we feel."

The occasional use of "I" reminds your audience that you are both the architect and the artful interpreter of information. Of course, you can be part of a team. There's a rhythm to being "we," to not grabbing acclaim. But since women err so much in the other direction, it's important to understand that failing to say "I believe," or "I don't agree," or "I'll do it" is forfeiting a moment to lead. "We," for example, may be inclusive; it may be an accurate description of how the work was done, but there's little personal presence in the group-think implied in "we" . . . or accountability for that matter.

When the teams at Ogilvy turned to peer at their fact-crammed power point presentations, I would urge them to start over and open their presentation with a hand-lettered chart that featured only one or two provocative words. That way, the audience couldn't go into reading mode and had to wait for the speaker to interpret these few words. That's where I wanted the team—out in front and in control of the information which was being received.

As we reviewed our women's skilled but personally neutral presentations, we realized they were actually dodging the spotlight, standing to the side, lowering the lights (after all, the power points have to look bright), and using a reporter's voice ("just reporting the facts, ma'am").

> You'll never communicate the most evocative aspects of your self-portrait if you aren't willing to step out in front of the work.

A Guide to Presenting

I developed a guide for how to put yourself, your insights, wisdom, and distinctive traits up front, in full view.

Begin in the Middle

Open with a sweeping idea or the most interesting fact or conclusion. Buried in every presentation is the point of greatest interest or at least one surprising element. Start there, out of order, and then spend the rest of the time defending that eye-opener. It creates tension, it's not predictable, and it forces you to state and then support a conclusion. Whose voice is being heard? Yours. Not the drone of the facts or the charts or the rules.

A researcher at Ogilvy discovered that the color yellow was why the guys preferred Ryder moving trucks to U-Haul. She did not begin her presentation as usual, describing the people interviewed, ages, frequency of use of Ryder, the twenty questions asked, and so on. Instead, she put up a chart with the word "yellow" on it and then explored its significance to the users of Ryder trucks. Then, with a second chart, she used a quote: "I remember my first shiny red truck. I loved that truck."

Now that she had her audience intensely curious, she was in complete control of the pacing. She was not doling out the results of the research in one power point slide after another, leaving the audience to decide what it all meant. Whether or not they eventually read the supporting documents, her audience did not forget this presenter or her conclusions.

Find the Drama

In the presentation, find the people who make up dry regulations, the laws, find the drama behind the numbers, or the facts. All over the world there are studies about what people eat, get sick from, live in, want to do, drive, wear. In these studies, individuals are reduced to numbers. Put people back in your presentations by using tapes of them speaking, photographs, or quotes (even ungrammatical ones).

If you're thanking people in the room, put their pictures on the screen—it will wake them up. Quote directly from the CEO's speech. That puts him or her in the room too.

Alexandra brought the drama of real life into an overly formal, somewhat hostile discussion. Alexandra was part of a team presenting its credentials to a hospital group. The deciders were an uneasy mix of legislators and physicians who played a big role in regulating the hospitals.

It was all so stiff and formal; all the information they requested made our charts so complex, and they dictated the agenda down to the last minute. I felt as though we had all forgotten why we were there. When we were halfway through, I set my charts aside and said, "I almost died in your hospital a year ago. Without the skills and care of a staff that had access to state-of-the-art equipment, my two daughters would have been motherless."

Alexandra had a deep personal involvement in this "product," and she was not afraid to show it. Of course her team won, because all of the presenters after her also presented the real life of a hospital breaking out of an overly formal format. Try reminding everyone "why we came here in the first place" to wake up a leaden agenda.

> Dare to bring the drama and energy of real, raw life back into a dry presentation.

Use Unexpected Visuals

Borrow shamelessly to open up the density of the material. I knew a man who collected wild cartoons for this purpose. People couldn't wait for his presentations. Try music, sound effects, anything to get out of your rut. Lots of customers and clients have mandated formats, but you can always have one or two custom touches that expand the idea or remind the viewers of the life around the issues at stake.

Account executives get stuck making fact books for their clients' brands. Roger didn't believe they ever read them, even though they took weeks of work to put together. In his most recent tome, he inserted a treasure hunt, complete with clues, on page 20 to page 24, but he held back the solution: the treasure was a little known market fact. He got a call from the CEO of Oscar Meyer. When he heard the name, he thought someone was kidding him, but it really was Mr. Bryan. He congratulated Roger for bringing wit and a wider perspective to the hot dog business.

Let Silence Develop

I used to think a seamless flow was the mark of a good presenter, but I learned that a deliberate pause, a hesitation, returns an audience from its wanderings.

I asked a speechmaking expert to give the public diplomacy representatives from the State Department some advice on public speaking. The teams reporting to me when I was the undersecretary of public diplomacy included people stationed in every embassy around the world. I organized our first-ever sales conference in Washington, D.C. The speech teacher wanted three days to deliver her lessons, but we cut her to one hour. So she was forced to zero in on the crux: "There's nothing as effective to bring your audience back as a moment of silence." And then she stopped. Everyone, especially the ones woolgathering, looked up and began to listen.

You don't have to be at the podium. You can say in a meeting, "I'd like to comment on that" and pause, and the room's attention will shift toward you. It is hard to do this, but it's worth the risk. At the very least you will be recognized as thoughtful.

Avoid Predictable Sequences: Next, Next, Next

This includes not telling the group what you're going to tell them and not noting how long your talk will take. This is a dreadful habit some speech teacher passed along in the 1940s.

If people think "I always know what Jan is going to say," you have become way too orderly in giving out your information. Since people are reading their emails and shuffling papers as conversations flow around them in meetings, you need to replace predictability with anticipation or anxiety; or let them know what you expect them to do or comment on. "Joe, I'll ask you to comment on one area." That's why the old threat "and I'll be asking questions at the end" works so well: it gives your audience a direct assignment, anticipation, a little anxiety.

Draw an Implication

The minute you interpret the flow of information, you make yourself present. When you offer your own view, you are giving them yourself. You are not a robot. They can read the charts, the regulations, the numbers, the study without you. Your job is to try to say what it all means. Even if you only have an opinion starter as a complex issue unravels, you have been the one who fielded the first ball.

Think About Your Voice, Your Vocabulary

If your voice trails up at the end of a sentence or at the conclusion of a segment, you are indicating doubt rather than showing resolve. *Let your voice reflect the power of your personal conviction.*

Avoid telling rather than showing; as in: "I'm so very excited to be here." Exaggerated claims about the depth of your feeling leave people uneasy, especially early in a presentation. Show your involvement or your intensity as the presentation unfolds. Try "I believe." It has to be used sparingly, but it is a way to show your total commitment.

"You'll find this is an amazing [finding/product/test/result/event]." You are presuming your listeners' own response. This is telling, asserting a conclusion your listeners need to come to on their own. Your audience will respond privately, "Well, I'll be the judge of how amazing it is." Give them the chance to discover for themselves how amazing it all is, as you deliver the great reveal.

Tell a Story About Yourself

This can be a simple aside or a quick illustration, or it may feature you as a witness rather than the heroine. After years of practice at presenting myself and Tatham's work to discriminating audiences, I found myself facing the toughest audience ever. As the brand-new chairman of the American Advertising Association of America (called the 4A's), I was making the keynote welcome to the audience made up of agency heads of vast worldwide enterprises.

Although CEO of Tatham, I was younger than most of them and from a smaller agency (in the Midwest, no less). Since I was the first-ever female chair of the organization, I was really anxious to show my gravitas.

As soon as I got to the podium, before I said a word, my right earring fell off, clattered against the mike, and rolled onto the floor. Everyone snapped to attention. I saw that my knuckles were white against the edge of the podium. I looked up and found this way out: "Well, that's one problem your previous chair did not have," I said, "I think I can still talk with one earring, but now I understand why the 4A's staff sent me a memo offering to change the chairman title to chairchick. Chairbroad is under consideration too." My elite audience laughed in appreciation, but I relaxed myself and them by giving them a story of how we were dealing with the "first woman" issue.

Beyond Informing to Asking

Though these guidelines will make you a better "informer," the more important presentation for women to master is learning to ask—in routine matters, about being included, certainly in regard to money matters or about your promotion or estimate of your potential.

> What we are willing to ask is a mirror of our self-esteem and the expectations we hold for ourselves.

Every feature you've placed in your portrait delivers a message to you about what you should ask, or what cannot be allowed to go unchallenged. Alice's two portraits set in motion new priorities. Consider what she's asking of herself with these different self-images. *From* "I see myself as a flooding plain; everyone is irrigating off my waters" *to* "I am a mighty river, bounded by trees and mountains, directing my own current."

To become a mighty river of a manager, Alice will have to reintroduce herself by asking others to see her anew. Her first target is her boss. His casual remark in the big annual meeting about how he saw her never left her thoughts during the portrait exercise. She recalls that he said, "Alice just does anything we ask of her."

"In that meeting, I was in the low flood zone, no particular point of view, with no project for our office. I was just seeping along."

She asked him for a follow-up meeting, the first private one she'd ever had, at their headquarters in Washington. She brought him an idea for a nationwide project. "Our office can initiate a study of how women use our health care services after they've had surgery. There's no such information on women, only on men." Then she added, "This will be perfect for you to refer to in the panel you're chairing on the government's interest in women's medical issues."

Alice was surprised at how quickly he signed on. "He even gave me a research team to help. I didn't know the company even had a team like this."

Alice followed an approach to asking that is usually successful and keeps the asker on point:

She asked for his undivided attention in a
     one-on-one.
She brought an idea; she didn't whine
     about not being given a group project.
She made it relevant to him (his panel).

> There is an approach, an underlying pattern, to successful asking.

A Proposition

I can trace the turning point of my success at Tatham to when I learned how to ask for the right thing in the right way, using that very same process. I was late in my first year there and the senior partner on our Proctor & Gamble business. I really knew Head & Shoulders shampoo well, the product that was viewed as the mother lode of profits and prestige at Proctor. Tatham was on probation, so I did not to ask to be introduced to John Smale, the CEO of P&G, until I knew our team had some solutions for Head & Shoulders.

As my two partners, both big, athletic men, introduced me to John Smale, they joked that women (like me) were a lot of trouble. For example, I didn't pick up the lunch tab, didn't play golf. John smiled at me with what I took to be compassion. Then they promptly launched into an animated discussion about fishing, something all three men loved. When I saw John glance at his watch, I clutched at the arms of my chair; I hadn't said a word. So I broke right into the trout story.

"Mr. Smale, I learned when I was on a competing shampoo brand (this established my credentials with a tempting opening)" John leaned forward, the fish forgotten. "Also we've just discovered (I gave him a present, an important insight the company didn't have) which has led us to a new idea for Head & Shoulders." He had once worked on the H&S brand; he couldn't resist. "I promise to keep you posted." (The rumor was that John liked to be in the loop.)

And then came the big ask: "May I call you next week? I have a proposition for you." That's a woman's tactic. Never say to a man, "Can we talk?" But a proposition, that's intriguing. My buddies were open-mouthed as John agreed to a private meeting.

After we left, I explained my proposition. If, and it was a big if, we increased the sales share of Head & Shoulders with our new TV campaign, I wanted John to give Tatham a new brand as an overt show of support, preferably soon.

At our private meeting, John carefully explained that it wasn't their policy to react quickly to sales improvements, but then he gladdened my heart with his parting words. "I promise you, I'll think about it."

Our new marketing campaign increased Head & Shoulders' sales share, and five months later, we were given a new laundry cleaner assignment. It was the first new brand Tatham had been awarded in four years, and it was a signal heard loud and clear, especially in our halls: Tatham was off probation.

Asking Has a Pattern

Here's the pattern revealed in this little playlet: I had *studied my receiver*. I knew his history, his inclinations, his biases, and a few rumors. I started with our *common ground*. We both had a great interest in this shampoo. I brought a *present*. A newly discovered consumer insight that led to a tantalizing prospect of a big campaign for Head & Shoulders. I kept it *relevant to his interest*. *I spoke quickly*, eliminating anything that was extraneous, so I could ask him for a private meeting the following week. Granted, this next meeting, the second ask, was a much bigger one, but I hate to think how long it would have taken me to get another audience with John without this first request.

The word "proposition" was carefully chosen. Imagine his guarded response if I'd said "favor." A proposition implies that there will be an interesting exchange of mutual advantages.

In that second meeting, I was offering a benefit. A newly revitalized, highly motivated agency is exactly how P&G believes big brands are built. If he had said no, neither I nor the agency would have been damaged; at the least, we would have earned a little higher recognition, maybe begun to reset a drab reputation.

Artful asking includes all of these:

- Know and respect your receiver.
- Find a common ground.
- Present some kind of gift.
- Remind your listener that there's a benefit in agreeing to this "ask."

SHEILA GETS A RAISE

Sheila had already struck out twice at trying to get a raise. She said it was like shadowboxing with a ghost because her boss, Margaret, agreed that she deserved a raise. Margaret insisted she had asked but couldn't get approval.

Sheila laid out her options, following the crux exercise. She set aside the fear she'd get only a menial raise, her skepticism about how hard Margaret had really tried, and her anger that she made $4,000 less than her direct reports. She decided the crux was that she had to motivate Margaret to be the big asker. Sheila asked for a meeting after work.

She delivered her gift right away by telling Margaret that a reporter was doing an article on how young leaders lead, and Sheila had recommended Margaret as the perfect person to interview She knew Margaret was proud of her ability to look out for her team.

Sheila got to the core message by confessing to Margaret that she was disappointed in their company, wondering if they took seriously what they promised about values and recognition. "I mean, Margaret, if even you, their management of the future, cannot get a proven performer like me a raise of $10,000 (which just gets me to the norm), then what do you and I have to look forward to . . . what's the message to us?"

Not surprisingly, Margaret's face stiffened and she started closing her briefcase. Sheila knew she had to sit tight. Part of asking is bearing the tension of letting your proposal just hang there. Those awful minutes when you want to take it all back because the listener is surprised or reluctant. Hang on, look interested, sit still.

Sheila remembered her friend Grace's story to help her sit tight. When Grace wants to encourage her sons to feel free to discuss sex with her she sits still. "No matter what they ask, I don't wince. I never move a muscle. If they see me wince, it's over."

Margaret, almost out the door, turned back to Sheila and said, "Let me have another go at it."

Sheila got her raise. It was a good one. She also helped a victorious Margaret become more of a real leader. That was the benefit to Margaret: she was emboldened by Sheila's way of asking her to act for both of them.

Ann Lamott, a wise essayist and novelist I admire, could have been describing Sheila when she commented in a 2009 article in Oprah's magazine, "In the end, the answer to 'who are you meant to be' is perhaps this: the person who keeps asking the question." The operative verb is "asking."

Beyond Asking to Confronting

Confronting is asking on steroids. We all have different thresholds of tolerance for work situations that inspire overt anger such as dishonest or incompetent decisions, a severe loss, or personal attacks. Confronting someone or something requires facing the problem directly with pointed action. It is necessary only when all the other alternatives—waiting it out, forgetting it, giving it to someone else—don't work; in other words, when all other options stink. At that point, action is so essential that it becomes a form of bravery. We have to learn how to endure a frontal confrontation.

Some relationships are so problematic that you have to either yield up too much of yourself or resolve to confront the problem. I believe in moving toward the problem. While a few such problems may fade away on their own, most will just get worse.

CELIA AND THE BULLY

Celia normally handled her bully of a boss by giving in to his every demand and almost cowering when his voice deepened and his face reddened during one of his angry fits. Sometimes she and her team weren't even the target. Even as he raged on at someone else, Celia would still be the one shaking. Her reaction was physical. Dana was 6 feet 4 and Celia was 5 feet 2. She was a slender, dark-haired woman, her soft voice belying a first-rate brain and, as you'll see, a steely side. She and Dana were teamed in a high-pressure retail organization. In retail, tomorrow is too late. Dana used this urgency to insist that a complex report had to be completed in only two days. Celia knew it would take at least a full week's worth of work.

Celia had been working on her presentation skills and decided to challenge Dana's reign of terror. But as she entered his office, she completely forgot the rules of asking and confronting. She slapped his memo on the desk and said, "We can't give you this by tomorrow; that's not enough time." Dana leaped up so fast from his chair it fell over with a horrible crash to accompany his shouting.

"I hate that he stood up. Now he was a giant again, but in the middle of all the bedlam, it hit me: this is his anger, it's not mine. I do not have to take it on." So she just stood, silently waiting, and when his bluster showed signs of ebbing, she delivered her message. "I can't hear you in all this yelling, Dana. Call me when you've calmed down . . . because I know you need this report."

Celia realized that the last part—that the report was essential for him—was her leverage, a present in reverse, and their common ground. "He can have his fit, but he can't have the report. It's that simple," she reported. Alas, Dana did not become a balanced human being, but he did have fewer victims because petite Celia took him on and won.

Turning Confrontations Around

Sometimes the situation is reversed, and someone is confronting you. You can manage the confrontation by being frontal or by learning these two ways to respond: (1) turn sideways or (2) underreact. I must admit, I have rarely pulled off the latter, but it's very effective.

I have had wise teachers who counseled handling hot attacks or disagreements by turning sideways, making a mental (or physical) move to avoid an unproductive hostile or overly aggressive event face on. The experts who teach people how to safely manage hostile or tricky TV interviews use this form of indirect response. No matter what the interviewer challenges you with, such as "I understand you voted for the bill two years ago that you are now fighting," you, as the responder, turn the conversation toward your interest, such as "Yes, the way I feel about this bill now is influenced by . . . "

POWELL TURNS SIDEWAYS

In the business world, giving a swift answer to a direct question is a mark of being on your game, so I had a hard time trying to figure out how to deal with tricky questions from the press when I was working at the Department of State. Secretary Powell showed me a whole other way to handle confrontations when he interrupted my first-ever press conference to discuss breaking news about a treaty with Russia. I was scheduled to show a ten-page booklet tracking the interconnecting web of terrorism, but the press got a lot more excited when word got out that Powell would be there. I almost fled the room when I saw thirty cameras lined up at the back like big black eyes recording my maiden voyage as a State Department presenter.

Secretary Powell, who didn't get to be a general by avoiding confrontations, began his briefing in his usual calm, succinct manner, speaking about a missile containment agreement the United States had just signed with Russia. To my surprise he offered to take a few questions from the press.

The reporters began firing pointed, complex, and leading questions. I watched Powell carefully because he didn't seem to be hearing the questions. When a reporter asked him about the diamond trade in Africa, Powell just made another point about the treaty with Russia. Later that day, I tracked him down to ask why he didn't answer the reporters' questions. He smiled and said, "Well, you know, I told them I'd take questions, but I never promised to give answers [a sideways move]. I often choose not to answer certain questions. Other times, I cannot, for security

reasons. Remember that during those press conferences, the cam-
eras are on me. I'm talking to the world, not to just one reporter
trying to get his story."

That was a two-part lesson for me:

- First, a challenge doesn't always deserve or need a frontal response.
- Second, be very sure who your true audience is.

A sharp, disruptive question in a meeting can distract you from the larger purpose of your message. So don't answer it. Instead, turn side-ways, toward what you want to say.

Reframe the Confrontation

Secretary Powell was also a master at reframing a question to suit his own purposes (another form of turning sideways). A reporter once asked him why he had chosen me, a Madison Avenue type, described by him as a "seller of rice," to conduct public diplomacy. My more recent history of shepherding huge world brands like Ford, IBM, or American Express would have been harder to mock, so the reporter went back thirty years to my youthful career at Uncle Ben's Rice to define my career. Rather than challenge or correct the reporter, Powell diverted the question. "Well, you know, Uncle Ben's is in a lot of homes. If she can do that good a job for Uncle Ben's, I think she can help us here with our brand."

Turning sideways is a great way to defuse a challenge. You divert the speaker's intention by not responding at all or not responding in kind.

Underreacting is not looking away or letting the problem die of ne-glect; it is restraint and it is usually arrived at after you've privately ac-knowledged your fury and judged it to be irrelevant. When you're emotional, you want to dominate the action. Underreacting gives the other person a chance to modify his or her position. It's hard to do, but often smart to do.

The Morning After

The morning after I escaped from Howard, the client I had just met, who had trapped me in his Helmsley Hotel suite, I woke up feeling angry and frightened that there could still be blowback on me and Tatham.

> Here's the key to successful underreacting: leave the participant an important role to play.

What had occurred the night before was so wrong, so potentially dangerous, that I felt I was at fault too. I should never have gone up to that suite. I felt ashamed and blamed myself. What had I been thinking? I'd never let myself be cornered before. I knew all this spinning was irrelevant, but it swamped my thinking. I kept reminding myself that it had been our first meeting. He didn't even know me. Still, the crux was, I had to find a way to prevent this sordid event from sabotaging our biggest new account or tarnishing my reputation.

I called my three male partners at Tatham and related the whole sorry tale. They were outraged and wanted to retaliate in some way. "I think it's up to me to deal with this," I regretfully realized. "We can't let this fester. He's going to wake up panicked that I might try to bring him down, and, knowing his mentality, he will probably try to strike first."

When I said "knowing his mentality," I was referring to the little I knew of Howard's work style and vocabulary. He was known as a "quid pro quo" manager; it was important to him to create trade-offs, good-for-you, good-for-me deals. I had to find a way to speak to him in terms of reciprocity, but I had to do so right away. And I had to underreact.

My hand trembled as I punched his number into the telephone. It was not yet 7:00 AM. "Hello," he croaked.

"Howard, this is Charlotte." Silence. "You were not yourself last night."

"Oh, ah, I, er . . . "

"It could have been a nightmare for both of us."

"I know, I know," he muttered.

"It's impossible for me to continue to work with you, but our other managing partner will take over your account," I said. "The work we're doing together is more important than this episode." That was a pretty neutral summary, setting my fury aside. Next came the quid pro quo. "I expect this account change will be well received at your company, right?" I paused. "And Howard, I will never mention this; it's over."

He pondered my words, then replied in a halting but stronger tone. "Thank you." Howard had made a choice too. Tatham would be protected, I was offering him a pass.

The new team leader did well, and I never saw Howard again. It was quid pro quo. If I hadn't added my condition, "I expect this change to go well," he might not have heard so clearly the price of my restraint.

You are comfortable informing, but when you master the pattern of asking, you will not be tempted to avoid this more difficult form of communicating. Keep it in your tool kit at the ready, recognizing that there are times when you will also have to ask or manage a tough confrontation.

Informing, asking, and confronting are vital parts of persuasion, and knowing how to be persuasive is preparing you to lead.

9

IN CHARGE

When to Take the Lead

A VERY FEW people have such a strong internal compass that they know intuitively when to take charge. One of these rare creatures is Ina Garten.

In addition to an engaging laugh and an irresistible way with food, Ina's internal guide gives her flawless directions on how to invent and reinvent herself so successfully and so persuasively that everyone thinks she was their idea in the first place. It has guided her from her first invention, which was a store of delectable foodstuffs, to becoming a best-selling author and TV star. She makes it all look as easy as her recipe for lemon chicken. You might think that with such a well cali-brated compass, Ina would never feel lost. But she admitted to me, her faithful fan and witness to her many transformations, "Well, I'm always scared."

I find this apparent contradiction of Ina's inspiring . . . and true. Be-ing in charge of your work life doesn't mean you always move with as-surance and sublime self-confidence; it means you keep moving, continuing on your own path, even when you feel shaky and uncertain.

Ina created a food emporium called the Barefoot Contessa in East Hampton, New York. To shop there was an exhilarating experience.

The food was like jewelry, glowing and gleaming, wrapped in tissue, set in porcelain, displayed on wooden boards. We were all caught up in Ina's belief that great-looking and delicious food foretold a party about to begin. The store seemed to be an extension of Ina's personality, but when she sold it after a few years she felt quite lost.

Not long after that, she was invited to do a TV pilot. It sounded like a great idea. But Ina had developed such a deep sense of who she is and who she isn't that she walked off the set during the first TV test trial. "They wanted me to follow their format. I wanted to do what would be real for me," she said.

Her sense of self intervened again when she talked to a publisher about doing her first cookbook. Ina thought of her mission (what I would call her self-portrait) as a hostess having fun at her own beautiful party. Ina didn't like the idea for the cookbook that her publisher suggested. She didn't think a big tome of recipes marching one after the other looked like much of a party.

She did agree to do a book, but on her terms, breaking a lot of sacrosanct publishing rules in the process. Instead of ceding control to the publisher's art department, Ina paid for her own photographers and stylists, gambling the family nest egg on this first unproven book concept. She fought for a hand-painted decorative stripe on the cover, which proved to be a signature used in all of her following books. Most of the people on the publishing team questioned her innovations. The only friend she had at the company, inspired by Ina, said, "Hey, just get out of her way." That's what being in charge sounds like.

The doubters and naysayers were vocal throughout the process of making Ina's cookbook. A prominent food critic wrote that a cookbook with so few recipes would never succeed. Since the book sold over 100,000 copies in its first year alone, I imagine that critic seldom refers to her scathing review.

Ina then took her unique template to television. She knew which TV producer, a woman from England, she wanted to use. By this time she was an established author, and her producers at the Food Network moved swiftly to make this happen. Now Ina is the adored "big sister" to everyone who watches her show. She continues to invent herself in new arenas such as food products for supermarkets, but it all has to feel like a party to her . . . and to us, her fans.

Recently I caught up with Ina on the phone when she was in Los Angeles. I asked her if anyone there had asked for a hug, as her fans often do. That great laugh bubbled up and she said, "No, but Tony Bennett, whom I've never met, just yelled across the pool to me, 'Hey Ina, I love your meatballs.'"

By the way, it was Martha Stewart who helped Ina find the experts she needed to pull that first cookbook together. I love this example because it bodes well for the time when women will be found more and more at the top and will be generous enough to lend a hand to other women.

Recognizing the Moment to Lead

It is so easy to dodge or miss a moment when you need to up your game at work. It is important to know just when taking charge is good for you, when you might later regret not going for the brass ring. If you believe the world will be a better place because you have both the desire and the means to take charge, that's the time for you to jump in. It doesn't matter if you rise up to take the lead only once or twice in your entire working life or if you do it daily. There are so many moments when you can make a difference—by enriching an outcome, saving a great idea, defending the beleaguered or downtrodden, and, not least, expressing your own gifts and wisdom.

It is profoundly depressing to leave a room saying to yourself, "I wish I'd said that," or to watch a group that you could have guided fail, or to realize that you bailed on yourself. These are moments of leadership lost.

Look for these signals that reveal a leadership moment:

- You become inflamed.
- You want to initiate change.
- You're willing to persuade others to accept that change.

If you don't care strongly about an issue, you won't have the power to stay the course. Others don't have to like your idea; they only have to be convinced it's going to happen. And if they're positive about it, well, that's a plus. Caring deeply, feeling that it matters greatly, will encourage you to risk stirring up the situation. It's very important to know how to make an intelligent and effective fuss. That's what all the communication disciplines I've outlined are for. By now you have the discipline to be clear and to say what you mean, even when you are disturbed, angry, or fiercely determined. Unless you channel those feelings into an ability to persuade others that your ideas are necessary, perhaps inevitable, your fierce feelings will only alarm your colleagues.

> If you don't have an impassioned belief that where you're leading is essential, you will falter and be overwhelmed by resistance from others.

Here is the dirty little secret about being in charge: in the short term, it's often not much fun. Being in charge of an agreeable and like-minded team is nice, but it's not leading. It's managing. Most of us are not looking for a fight, so it is satisfying to direct a highly motivated team to a consistent set of objectives. The trick is to know when even managing well is strangling your conviction that something needs to change.

When I told Ina Garten about someone who constantly second-guessed me when I was at the State Department, she said, "Everyone tries to throw you off your game." I never forgot this reminder that I had to both identify and defend "my game."

There is a difference between your daily life of getting the job done and the exceptional moment of stepping into the lead, defending your game. Granted, it takes a lot of concentration to present your truest, largest self in the fast-moving, largely indifferent modern workplace. If that's all you do, you will still be significantly enlarging your life at work. You will be making a difference. You'll be better at most work relationships, inspire others to collaborate, know when and how to defend your team, and make smarter hiring and firing decisions. It's no small accomplishment to be an authentic manager. Leading, though, requires a degree of passion and intensity that you don't normally express in your day-to-day role.

> We all need to learn to manage, but I hope you'll discover that you have a need and the capacity to take the lead.

Fanning a Spark into a Flame

Whenever you have had to confront someone, you have responded to a spark that ignited you long enough to take a stand.

That spark has to become a flame when you focus on the larger task of leading others. You have to pursue your convictions past reasonableness, toward an unknown outcome that only you can envision.

I'm making this sound like an event the size of a world war, but in truth, a moment of leadership can be small. These moments usually revolve around change, often disruptive change. If you dare to be a change agent, you will find yourself called upon to persuade others to do something uncomfortable—reverse a position or perhaps stop cold—in order to create a new order.

> A new, unproven vision will not usually be comfortable or welcomed in the short term.

Maybe you don't want to face that kind of disruption every day, but please don't lose your moment to take the lead just because you're afraid to be forceful or persuasive or feel reluctant to let a spark fan into a flame.

The lure of just going along in the slipstream of work is the greatest flame extinguisher. Although few will admit to being conformists in today's workplace, most prefer to "go along," to stick to their own turf, which is familiar and manageable. As a manager you will be applauded for fostering the peace or smoothing over conflicts. Women naturally err on the side of accommodation. In all my workshops, this pressure to be accommodating is discovered as a limitation.

> WOMAN 1: If I step out in favor of this better way of doing things, everyone else will be uncomfortable.
> WOMAN 2: God forbid you should make anyone uncomfortable, right?
> WOMAN 1: Well, if I do just go along, I sign up to be miserable myself.
> WOMAN 2: We're talking about these changes because we're upset with the status quo. If someone has to be upset, why does it have to be me, sitting here frustrated and silent?

These women are saying that seeking to persuade others and to change things is not a onetime act that shakes everything up and then peace is restored. You have to be able to endure the friction that you could avoid by being more accommodating.

Does It Matter to You?

That's why you have to be very clear that the stakes matter to you and that you are stepping out for a mighty purpose. When I decided not to react to the "evil cabal" that was planning a mutiny at Ogilvy, our follow-up meetings about our unproven vision took on an almost unbearable level of tension. It would have been a great relief to call out the ringleader of the mutiny, but I needed to direct my energy toward persuading the people who did want to create a new Ogilvy. So I sat tight and bore the tension. I could do this only because I believed that this change would knit Ogilvy back together again.

It can be difficult for women to overtly seek to influence others. It appears to be modest and far less risky to give everyone all the facts and then step politely aside while they come to their own conclusions.

I have had to really battle this tendency among many women to favor provables over the riskier game of leading toward a new frontier. For example, Sam, our "brain in the jar" digital talent, preferred to dazzle everyone with the facts. Her favorite stepping-aside technique was to lay out a dizzying mountain of complex steps and then pronounce the conclusion *self-evident*. Excuse me? Things that are self-evident don't need you or the presentation anyway. Relying only on logic, on what can be factually established, may inform or intimidate, but it will rarely stir anyone into action or change.

Whenever a woman pleads fiercely for change, she risks being labeled self-aggrandizing or, more wickedly, a self-promoter. My seminars make it clear that some of the first negative reactions to your taking charge will come from other women. "It brings out our well-known passive-aggressive tendencies. These women claim they want to help my cause, but then they whisper to others that I'm disruptive, a troublemaker," Rachel, the former Little Red Riding Hood, said bluntly.

> The world is quick to label women leaders as pushy and self-aggrandizing until the results are so good they're impossible to ignore.

A woman who created a powerful voice in critiquing current political events was labeled by other women: "She is like every other professional feminist, dedicated to promoting herself." This woman who created a new arena for political discourse was called a "shameless self-promoter" but became a "media visionary" when she successfully took her company public. There is nothing quite like the hard evidence of having pulled it off to overcome such labels.

At Ogilvy I was declared to be "in over my head" and a "mammoth ego," until our success was irrefutable; then I was called a "charismatic leader."

MARGARET THE MISSIONARY

Margaret ignited a flame, in spite of herself, over one long night of work. Margaret was a newly minted manager, but she didn't love her new role. "They want me to drive, but they haven't given me the keys," she said. Margaret's company made software that tracked complex financial and legal transactions, but it required much explaining and instruction to use. Margaret was promoted by Mike to interface directly with her customers.

Unfortunately, Margaret didn't feel like selling was as satisfying as being an expert. "Mike tells me I have to be a missionary for the cause," she said. "He means I should deliberately lead these customers, close the deal, even as I instruct them as to what our software can do. I never liked the missionary position," she joked, but I could see she was seriously thinking this client manager role wasn't for her.

A month later, Margaret was still grumbling to me about not being clear about her duties. As she was speaking, Mike came into the room to congratulate her on the big win. Margaret explained, "We have a real weird client. He comes to work at 5:00 PM in the afternoon and stays in the finance department all night by himself. When I finally met with him, it was so frustrating; it was clear he didn't think our software could do the job. So I called home, canceled dinner, and stayed into the wee hours with him till I convinced him he had more to learn."

"Well, what happened?"

Margaret said rather offhandedly, "Oh, he bought the whole package, the service, and some hardware too."

I looked hard at her. "Well, you must have been pretty convincing."

"I wasn't trying to be persuasive," Margaret said. "I was just so furious that he didn't get it, that there were big gains for them that he couldn't see. I could not leave until I converted him."

Margaret had fanned a spark into a flame. She may be a world-class expert on the logic of how this software works, but she had to put something of herself, her own beliefs, on the line to convince her reluctant client. She didn't want to be a "missionary" and didn't think of herself as "persuasive," but by canceling dinner, by refusing to quit, she was stepping into a moment of leadership, changing her role and how her client viewed her.

Leading Requires Persuasion

Taking part in the adventure of persuading others, sweeping them up into the vision, is a wonderful experience. The ability to create excitement all around you is what leadership is about. Listen to the sound of leadership; it is you being eloquent, powerful, convincing, compelling, and forceful. It is not for the faint of heart, but it is the inevitable outcome of caring a lot, of igniting a spark that grows into a flame.

> You are not trying to sway people against their will but to offer them a chance to see things anew.

Leading through persuasion is a way of communicating that must be learned. In fact, it has to be learned, for if you can't persuade or convince others, you cannot lead.

It helps to focus on the response you hope to evoke as a way to counter your own reluctance to ask others to change. Of course, laying out the response you want is part of your discipline in good communication, but in the goal of leading others, you are after one very specific response: "I never thought of it that way."

To elicit an "I never thought of it that way" response, you must be prepared to express your own excitement, your keenness, the leaps you've made from logic to an imaginative new idea, the size of which is yet unknown.

What new tools can you use to persuade others, to change people's minds? Imaginary flights, hyperbolic language, music, drum rolls? Well, maybe. But there are higher forms of communicating you are now ready to consider.

To create change, to invent a new future, you have to be vulnerable, to show passion and belief in an unproven idea, and to risk failure by pursuing it. You, the initiator, have to find a delivery style that allows you to communicate your conviction in a compelling, inescapable way.

Tools That Help You Lead

When your goal is to have more impact, when the force of your presentation will alter things, you have to deliver your message with such a high degree of fervor that it overwhelms your audience's resistance. You may need to deflect skepticism, shake away reluctance to embrace a new idea, or break through indifference.

In order of ascending artistry, here's a list of tools that I've seen leaders use to carry the flame:

Threats or consequences
Passion, pathos
Humor, wit
Imperfection
Surprise
Wonder

Threats or Consequences

Inertia or complacency can be converted into action by force, threat, or intimidation. This is why every enterprise has a bully or two. As a manager in a team, the agreed goals are usually incentive enough to get things going. But if someone falls behind or a faction resists, then you need to find a way of taking the lead.

You may find this shocking, but a common technique for getting the lead is to be threatening; to ramp up the urgency of what's at stake so the laggards get in line. Many men rather admire a terrorizing boss because they see the boss's bullying as proof of his belief and fervor, which they respect. They probably feel like they've just switched from their football coach to their business coach.

At least half of the executive women in my seminars have had someone rate them as intimidating. Their consumer research included comments like "aggressive" or "suffers no fools." This is part of the territory we women take on when we are in charge. Many people still find it uncomfortable to have a woman directing things, making strategic decisions, and declaring, "Let's take that hill." Many women find more palatable ways to get agreement, but they should never forfeit their hard-earned power to jump-start something by leading even less than nicely.

> Niceness won't be missed if you speak confidently from your certain knowledge that this matters to you.

You will develop your own way of exercising authority. Once you've mastered speaking clearly about serious consequences, you won't have to bluff or threaten or be a supplicant to convince anyone you mean business.

Carolyn, who is reshaping her way of working to resemble a dolphin rather than an octopus, found that her juniors thought of her as a shark. Only half in jest, Carolyn said, "Maybe I better pull back on the way I make demands. Even though these are the baby sharks and they'll eventually appreciate my intensity, they deserve more examples of how to be persuasive when they mean business."

Delivering ultimatums or scary scenarios or flaunting your power over someone may work, but it is not nearly as sophisticated a way to be in charge as inviting them to join you in a full-hearted commitment to a mighty enterprise. An invitation must be backed by the consequences of saying no. That's when the conviction of the one in charge shows she is prepared to be strong, forceful, even compelling, another side of being willing to take charge.

I had to draw a line in the sand at Ogilvy. I knew it might feel threatening to some, but I had to accept that.

Point of No Return

After we'd listened to everyone's ideas, revised our brand concepts, and succeeded with a few clients, the top people at Ogilvy were still debating the merits of brand stewardship. I called a special meeting to bring this fragmented bunch together. We had to have closure so we could go forward united. Instead, the meeting threatened to produce "death by debate." Also we were in an awful, hermetically sealed hotel and conference center, and our "closure" included name-calling, heavy drinking, and fistfights. The final dinner felt like the last supper. Early on the last day, I carefully reviewed how we got to our vision, why I believed it would work, and what we had learned about its value. Then I laid out the consequences:

> I have heard it said that in any big change, such as this new venture of ours, one-third of the people sign on wholeheartedly, one-third sit on the fence, and one-third never join in. I'm in the first group. Where are you? Because if you're not in the first third, you need to think about turning in your resignation. To make this work we are going to need the full weight of you our leaders moving with conviction and all your considerable talents behind brand stewardship. We can't afford any fence-sitters at the top.

I stiffened in anticipation, waiting for more debate; instead, a palpable energy filled the room and the group buzzed with excited talk. They were ready to go. This once reluctant, divided group knocked out a detailed plan for sending brand stewardship out far and wide, working as a strengthened and reunited Ogilvy.

Passion, Pathos

A story from the heart told well can change the response of everyone listening. It's persuasive because it is genuine.

Soldiers are not known for using pathos or evocative language, but consider how Colin Powell turned a hostile, cynical audience into a deeply appreciative one. In 2003, as our secretary of state, he spoke at Davos, Switzerland, to the World Economic Forum in a crowd that included a lot of people who were suspicious about the United States. He was greeted with respect, but the U.S. invasion of Iraq and our war in Afghanistan were controversial. There were heated discussions by the many religious, business, and political leader assembled there. After his speech, he got a tough question about when the United States should resort to hard power (military) versus soft power (diplomatic programs and dialogue). He paused to consider the question and then spoke from the heart, with the authenticity of a soldier rather than as a statesman.

"I have been a soldier for thirty-five years," he began. "It was not soft power that freed Europe in World War II. For the last hundred years, when the U.S. has sent our young men and women forth, many lives have been lost. We did not ask for treasure or land. We asked only for the ground to bury them in."

A venture capitalist friend of mine was there. He reported, "It was as though all the hard edges in the room and the tight faces softened—you could feel the change."

> Colin Powell persuaded his audience to make room for that other, larger picture of the United States.

To be eloquent like that, you have to be real; to be moved enough, informed enough, and maybe desperate enough not to worry about the cost of leading others to form a new picture, one that maybe only you can see.

Humor and Wit: The Great Liberators

You don't always have to heavy up on earnestness just to prove you care. You can use humor, a surprise to reveal a fresh perspective.

Humor is the most disarming ingredient for leavening the seriousness of work. I urge you to consider any avenue to humor that you and

> Humor carries goodwill and admiration; it invites others in.

your portrait can handle. Creative enterprises of any sort put a huge premium on humor because humor's cousins, irreverence and outrageousness, are great goads to opening up "I never thought of it that way" responses.

Humor is similar to the way creative departments in ad agencies use music. Anything that is too emotional to say, a deeply felt promise, a personal revelation, can always be sung. When it's put to music, it can be heard. Humor is a carrier like that.

AMY, LIZ, AND WHOOPI

I didn't expect to run into three examples of how to use wit, bawdy humor, and pathos at a single lunch. But I was in the company of some world-class persuaders. The annual Matrix Awards for women in communication are given to individuals who have found their own unique way of influencing their work world. The lunch would have been memorable for me because Katherine Graham, then the head of the Washington Post Company, offered to introduce me. I revered this woman, who had transformed herself from a homemaker into a leader as she shepherded the Washington Post to an even more influential voice.

When the novelist Amy Tan took the dais, she told us, in words spoken so quietly we had to strain to hear, how her life had been both shaped and haunted by her grandmother. This woman had felt so trapped, so restricted from having a life of her own in the China of her era that she took the only available way out: she committed suicide. Women in the audience were wiping their eyes as they listened intently.

Then Liz Carpenter approached the podium and waited until we looked up at her. As she stood there, the mood began to change. Liz was a well-known columnist, but this day, she stripped her credentials down to the basics, her throaty voice

clearly a little challenging: "I'm Liz Carpenter. What I do is . . .
I report gossip. Let me explain to you what gossip is. As Amy was
reducing you all to tears with her heartbreaking story, Whoopi
Goldberg, your next speaker, leaned over to me and muttered,
'Well, now, Amy has done it. The rest of us are truly fucked.'"
As laughter caught on and rolled out, Liz still had a punch line.
"That, my friends, is gossip."

Each speaker represented her own clearly defined self-portrait. Amy spoke movingly from the heart. Liz provoked with wit. And Whoopi startled us with humor. These are all persuasive ways of presenting who you are and evoking the response you want from the audience.

Imperfection Is Real

Perfection, in the form of a flawless stream of words delivered with cool composure, is never as persuasive as realness. An impassioned but imperfect speech, which shows you care too much to hide flaws, is far more compelling.

The story that Lillian brought to our private session is a familiar one for all of us women who are called "driven" or "hard-charging." This is a story about the pursuit of perfection that can be more self-destructive than influential. Lillian said:

PIT BULL

I am known as the persuader in the company. Anything that
needs turning around eventually comes to me . . . and I, by
sheer force of will, get the changes agreed to. But it's not as
satisfying as it used to be, and I see from my consumer re-
search that people feel more snubbed than impressed, even run
over. One of our company executives said to my boss, "Don't
send the pit bull over. I'll do it later."

"When did I get to be the pit bull rather than the talented per-suader?" Lillian asked me.

"Probably when you ceased to let everyone know how much this constant striving, this constantly hammering the stake in the ground, costs you as a mere human being," I answered. "Why not let your slip show a little?"

Lillian liked the slip metaphor. She liked the idea of showing she was normal, even imperfect. She surprised her team by confessing that a project discouraged her and asked for suggestions. "They were so dumbfounded, no one said anything, but I could see them looking at me in a more accepting way. Next time, maybe they'll join in when I let my slip show, when I don't have all the answers" was Lillian's new view.

Surprises Are Door Openers

Every chance you get, introduce the unexpected, an element of surprise.

Beers and a Pizzi

When I was at JWT, Carmen, my client at Sears, and I were told that a proposal we had for an ad budget for the portable drill would not fly. "Let it go. They'll never hear you."

Carmen Pizzi was the buyer, the marketing head at Sears, and I was his agency partner. He and I had chosen the Craftsman drill as the product ready for an advertising budget to bring before the all-powerful committee from Sears. The committee had rejected the drill three times before, and the coordinator thought we were crazy. "Same old, same old" was his way of brushing aside our request.

"But Carmen, this is no ordinary drill," I protested.

He smiled. In a weak moment, I had confessed to him that I had never held a drill in my life. He said, challengingly, "Show me." And I went through all I had learned about my beautiful drill.

Suddenly he had an idea. "That's it! We won't give them what they expect, so they can ignore it again. We'll give them a whole new delivery format, a surprise. You'll present the product. I'll present the ads about the drill."

The committee sat in a U, which felt like a coliseum designed for human sacrifice. Carmen invited the committee to have "Pizzi and Beer," a play on our names. No one smiled at this witticism. In fact, not a smile greeted me as I walked to the center of the gathering and looked Bob Anderson, definitely the ruler of this amphitheater, in the eye.

I could see they were disturbed that I, rather than Carmen, was up first. Their process was as sacrosanct as their seating plan. I began, "This is the world's best variable-speed, reversible, double-insulated drill." I took the drill apart to demonstrate "an armature field with solid brass ball bearings." I was an unexpected delivery agent, but I loved this drill and it showed. When I was done, Carmen presented the ads, dropped the boards, peered at the words. We were like a comedy routine; it was anything but dull.

"This concludes our presentation," said Carmen, motioning me beside him, taking a slight bow. King Bob stood and just looked at us. Was he about to leave in disgust? Then he began to clap. Soon all the men were standing and applauding. Our drill project was approved; the team of Pizzi and a Beer had not done a "same ole, same ole."

A refreshing slap of surprise runs through many of the successful ways there are to persuade others toward change and to cause an audience to respond more openly. Think of all the possible responses you can receive from your endless interactions with people, which unfortunately include lack of attention, distraction, and cynicism. These can be interrupted by a jolt, a surprise.

The Ultimate Surprise: Wonder

You can break down a mountain of indifference by learning how to communicate in a breakthrough way. The ability to say what you mean in its leanest form dramatically improves your chances of luring distracted audiences from ambient noise and the hypnotic draw of their messages and e-mails. But there are even bigger rewards if you can evoke wonder.

It's an unusual response, more of an occasional feat than an everyday exercise. The kind of wonder I'm talking about contains an element of surprise too. It is an important talent to be able to surprise people into wonder, as they often spend their whole working day trying to dodge unpleasant surprises. A good surprise is a welcome break.

Here's a way to train yourself to be drop-dead persuasive. Set as your goal (for a meeting, phone call, or presentation) that you will instill wonder to such a degree that your listeners respond, "Hey, I never thought of it that way."

Do you hear the wonder in this reaction?

You yourself can also be the source of wonder. In revealing to your audiences who you are becoming, you are presenting nothing less than a transformation. Transformations inspire wonder.

For the women in my seminars who become determined to present themselves on a bigger canvas, the response they actually did receive, time after time, was one of wonder. "Well, Morgan, I never thought of *you* that way."

I have talked to these bosses, men (usually) who were part of the target audience when the women presented their bigger self-portraits, and they are rather amazed at the difference in the women. "What has happened to little Celia? I can't call her 'little' anymore," one boss said. That's wonder.

Sometimes the audience may have a sense of wonder even if it makes them a little uneasy. "Alice just refused to fill in for me at that meeting. I always used to be able to count on her. What is going on here? Also, she's giving me grief about missing another meeting." That's Alice, the mighty river, being forceful and inspiring wonder.

Here's the boys' club response to Lydia the ice maiden: "Wow, can you believe it was Lydia who gave us that hilarious DVD? She was

blushing and laughing at the same time! That is not the Lydia we expected." That's wonder, even a little awe.

Think about the response Ina Garten got when she was working on
her first cookbook. She told the publishers she'd manage *and* pay for the
design, photography, and artwork. I imagine many people were amazed.
And what about that critic who predicted that a cookbook with so few
recipes, and such real ones at that, would be a complete flop? That same
book is in its twelfth year as a best-seller. I bet that critic is experiencing
wonder and a little humiliation.

With every step you take to be clear about your own place at work
and in every opportunity you seize to claim that place, you become
more of a leader. Such clarity is surprising and often impressive. When
Margaret worked through the night to convince her client of the merits of her company's software, she did not think of herself as trying to
lead him. She did not put on an artificial "let me talk you into doing
this" face. She was simply speaking from the center of who she was.

Speaking passionately from the very center of who you are is compelling, forceful, persuasive: that's what leadership sounds like.

10

CONTEXT
Where You Are

I CAME TO Ogilvy very clear that my role as a CEO and chairman was to be a change agent, to help this grand agency right itself, which would take untold changes and might prove beyond me. But at least I brought something valuable to the job in that I wanted to test myself, to see if I could put into practice on this larger canvas all that I had learned about marketing, brands, clients, people care, and motivation. That was my context. I didn't know how it would all turn out, but I felt I knew what WPP had hired me to do and why I wanted to be there. And then it all changed.

The context in which you view your work as well as the key people around that work can shift dramatically and leave you confused or, like me, in a funk.

I can pinpoint the very day when my job abruptly changed. It was in the early morning of my third year, on the way to IBM headquarters, summoned by Lou Gerstner, CEO of IBM. Lou wanted to "look us in the eye," "us" being me, Martin Sorrell, the head of WPP, and Shelly Lazarus—the head of Ogilvy North America.

At stake was the gigantic IBM advertising budget, estimated to be between $600 million and $1 billion. Lou had resolved to consolidate IBM's fifty-plus agencies from around the world into a single account at one big multinational ad agency. Ogilvy was their first choice, if we could win Lou's blessing this morning.

Lou and his sophisticated marketing head, Abby Kohnstamm, appeared in the small conference room. There was no casual chatting. Beneath Lou's polished exterior, a result of his elite résumé—Harvard, McKinsey Consulting, American Express, and Nabisco—was a very tough guy with one question, "How committed are you to IBM's success?"

It fell to me to answer. I acknowledged there was much at stake. IBM was at a crossroads with its own turnaround yet to be accomplished. I said we understood that IBM was gambling on Ogilvy's capacity to assume the work of many agencies and to successfully introduce IBM's new global vision. Then I paused and looked him in the eye. "We, however, are betting the future of our agency on this move."

I saw Lou lean forward and Martin stir in discomfort at the naked truth. Lou's eyes widened as I explained the staggering cost and discomfort to us of having to resign AT&T, Microsoft, and Compaq in order to clear conflicts for IBM.

After a good discussion, Lou gave us his blessing. The glow lasted all of ten minutes as we congratulated one another on this great adventure. The carefully choreographed announcement had to be made the next morning, as there were a lot of agency people working for IBM and our clients who deserved to get the bad news directly from the source. A tight band of tension settled in around my ribs as I returned to the car; the hard part was about to begin.

The review had been so closely held that few of our people knew. Command center was set up at my apartment. Jerry McGee, the account director of Microsoft, was waiting by the phone in Tokyo, Japan, for my "go" call. We had preset a meeting with Steve Ballmer, then number 2 at Microsoft. Jerry was so miserable at the prospect of firing his client that he was accompanied by an enforcer, Kelly O'Dea. They made an eloquent report on the size of the opportunity for us, and Ballmer, a very fair guy, simply said, "Under the circumstances, I don't blame you. I'd probably do the same thing." Whew. There were two more to go; it was a long day.

Even after winning the world's largest advertising account, we were still in the eye of the hurricane. We had to prove to ourselves and the world that we could do the job for IBM. *Business Week* magazine raised the question a lot of people were asking, "Was it worth it?" pointing out that IBM was in the midst of a wrenching restructuring, and carefully adding up the dollars we'd just forfeited from three big clients.

We got off to a rocky start with IBM. Even though we saw ourselves as very smart about brands, we were overwhelmed by the sheer size of IBM in the early briefings. A wall of work was falling on us, and we couldn't get a handle on what to address first. Our early ideas were too lofty, too stuffy, too old IBM. When we saw Abby's silent, disappointed face, we knew we needed to start over. We reread every comment in the brand research that our Ogilvy offices had conducted worldwide with their users and we discovered how to build IBM's before portrait. There was a bond between IBM and its users, but there was a glaring negative. Every user group acknowledged that the products and the technology were superior, but IBM could make it difficult to get help in using this complex technology. The before portrait was a big, black, impervious-looking fortress to reflect their isolation, along with a summary of the users' key question: We know you have the talent, but do you have the will?

Ogilvy's new portrait for IBM, the Solutions for a Small Planet campaign, turned out to be one of the most powerful brand statements ever launched, in fifty-eight countries simultaneously. Of course we had Lou's clarity, Abby's firm hand, and an amazing Ogilvy team headed by Shelly Lazarus, who figured out how to harness brand IBM.

When the IBM account was wooed and won, when Ogilvy proved up to the daunting task of communicating the new IBM, and our brand stewardship system had been delivered along with the IBM work, I realized with a sinking feeling that my job was over. With fourteen months to go on the five years I had promised Martin Sorrell, I had to accept that in swallowing IBM, the focus would move from building growth. The CEO job was not about big, bold change anymore. It was about our agency network, good management, follow-through. It was a big and challenging job, but now "change" wasn't as important as consolidation.

In the midst of the excitement about winning the largest ad account in history and the accolades that followed for our work, I had to fight off a serious funk. Seeing myself primarily as an agent of change, I felt cut loose from my moorings. I had completely lost context; why was I working?

What I needed to remember was that the motivations we have for working and what we expect to get from work are standard-bearers that we need to check in with when events move us to a different place.

In such shifts, you need to cultivate a sense of perspective that will enable you to keep track of where you are at work. I did ultimately realize I was simply moving into another life cycle in my work at Ogilvy and that my view of where I was had to catch up with reality.

The Penultimate Context: Why You Work

This is the big-picture issue: Why do you work? What do you want? Will your own needs shift and surprise you, or will the job morph into something so different you are left longing for the old days? (Which in our nanosecond world could be last week.) In order to be aware of this powerful frame of reference, you need to ponder your reasons for working.

When I was holding a summer seminar in East Hampton, Martha Stewart invited us to visit her. My career-focused women almost ran over me getting to the door. This was "Martha," their other teacher in so many ways, for so many years. As we sat on her rose bedecked, palest hue of aqua porch, spread around the steps and chairs with tea and cookies in hand, Martha began to speak. "Well, we are so glad Charlotte is working again. She needs to use that big brain" (as if I had been in a breadline).

Then she got serious. "My work is my life. My life is my work. There's no separation between the two." Martha is very clear on why she works. It's her life, and it's every single thing she touches, things that can be learned about more deeply and can be done well and can be shared with others. That's her perspective. The role that work plays in your life may be very different, but whatever that role is, it is part of the frame around your portrait.

That same day on the porch, Memrie Lewis, a landscaper and a close friend of ours for many years, spoke to the women about how we three had created our own small, loving family and told a few stories that had me wincing and the group laughing in surprise.

Later, when the women reflected, they wanted to use that tea party to refine their own idea of why they worked. Each one had a different perspective.

"I think all the time about the fact that Martha was forty-six when she started her magazine. I have time."

"I saw how the power of friendship lasted beyond the work with you three. I want that from my work partners."

"I *have* to learn to make those cookies."

"Why I Work" Camps

Women discuss their motivation for working in three general areas . . . when they think about it at all.

WHY I WORK

Camp 1: I have no idea.
Camp 2: I dream of a larger goal.
Camp 3: For the money.

If you feel ambivalent about why you are working, as Gwen did, that will dominate your experience. Gwen decided she could lead her big account if she could see herself as the conductor of a fine orchestra (although she's still gritting her teeth about being in the spotlight). She achieved this larger sense of herself by envisioning a new context.

Angie: Wave Walker

Angie made a career of never quite committing to work, much less to a vision of her own. In her first portrait, she called herself a "wave walker," tiptoeing along the tops of the issues, never sinking down into the grittiness of it all. Her previous boss had said, "Angie, you just have too many files open, on your computer, yes, but especially in the way you work."

Her dilettante's role, as she described it, was all flight and no fight. It came partly from her family of eccentrics who focused on the experiential, pulling Angie into a yearlong road trip just as she was taking honors in math class. She could bluff at work because she learned things so swiftly. But she had never learned how to hold the course.

She was stunned by an insightful comment from one of her interviews: "In lieu of your own plan, you follow someone else's, but lukewarmly." Angie knows her new portrait must reflect why she works—but she's not there yet.

One purpose of those after portraits is to reflect not only what it is you want to do today but in the long run also.

Sandy's Larger Goal

Sandy's before portrait was a mysterious woman in a cloak, and her after portrait was an uncloaked woman. The coat and hood reminded her that she needed to stop hiding her feelings and ideas as she artfully extracted everything others cared about. She was very astute at sizing up other people while never revealing anything about herself. Since she was a management consultant, this ability to disappear into the people and the problems she confronted was much admired. But Sandy wanted to take part rather than feel like she was a magnet attracting everyone's troubles.

In shaping her future portrait, removing the cloak was essential, but she set an even higher goal: "I've thought about why I work. I want to leave a legacy, a body of knowledge and understanding that will guide many companies in the future."

The word "legacy" puts Sandy's portrait into a bigger context. There is not one thing wrong with Sandy's job, salary, relationships—nothing she needs to change except this: she is not using her workday to include what she wants out of a life of working . . . to be a thought leader, to leave behind a legacy. She can begin now as she continues her work in human resources, continuing to study and create innovative manpower solutions as she goes. Every step she takes will now be affected by what she wants from work—a legacy that will outlive her own career and will affect how companies motivate and improve their people.

For the Money, Dummy

Candice was a strikingly good-looking woman in the New York workshop. She was wearing red stiletto heels with shiny black soles that caught the eye as she swung her crossed leg in a restless arc. She had a "don't mess with me" air, so it wasn't surprising to hear her spit out like a bullet the answer to the question of why she worked: "For the money."

She didn't have to add "dummy" because I could see a momentary flash of scorn on her face. It was replaced by a disarming smile that I imagine had worked well for her over the years. "Okay, we all work for money," I admitted. "That's real and it is our first reason, but what are your other reasons for working?"

She dropped her smile and said, "Reason 1 is money. Reason 2 is the money. Reason Number 3 is—would you like me to go on?

Red Shoes never made it to the portrait-making session because she was fired before our next meeting. She was vulnerable, particularly because she saw herself only as a paycheck; she didn't really like her work or her company. In this case, working for money was simply not enough.

Money Matters

Money is real. It's our first negotiation and can continue to be the most powerful measure of how we rate our progress. Money is part of why we work, but it can raise questions of self-worth or ramp up fears of lobbying for ourselves. It's important to put money in context too.

When I got a bonus, an unexpectedly big one (I'll never forget the amount—$8,000), I told a fellow at J. Walter Thompson who was a level above me. He never spoke to me again. I got the message. From that point on, I never wanted to enter a room with my salary preceding me. But WPP was a publicly held company, so my CEO salary was published. That was agonizing for me.

Shelly Lazarus, then our head of North America, gave me a fresh perspective on compensation. "We deserve it" is her straightforward view, completely free of apology or hedging. When she was a key player in a successful bid to bring in a whopper of an account, she told me, without an ounce of hesitation, that she had gone to the holding company, WPP, and asked for a big onetime bonus. "And I got it," she said, smiling.

I felt a thrill of surprise. Shelly's clarity and her timing knocked me out. She said it all with her last words, "I said to myself, 'If not now, when?'"

I really appreciate how open men are about deserving their money. They see money as an outward sign of how they're doing, a clear measure of how good they are. They're much faster to ask for it than we women are. As I began to earn big money, I wanted to be sure my salary package matched my peers', and it did. But I never felt that more and more money would make life better and better. Women have few people with whom to discuss this taboo subject. I once asked my trusted friend and lawyer, Phil Reise, how much money is enough. He answered in his own uniquely blunt way: "What you want is 'fuck you' money; enough money to walk away because at the top, where you are, the job can turn nasty and you may need to know you can always walk away. Then you don't have to, see?"

Most of us have to deliberately analyze how we feel about compensation. If you're contributing your time in charity work as many women are, holding our society together with all those "free" hours, the motivation for working (work that is every bit as demanding as what we paid workers do) is the belief that you're making a real contribution; it's psychic income.

> Putting money or recognition in its proper place requires you to respect the effort you make and assign a value to it.

You need to be very deliberate about placing an objective value on your energy and your commitment to the work, so you can influence others to do the same.

Role Reversal

I had a class of sixteen women who stumbled onto a completely new context in regard to women who work. It startled them and thrilled them a bit to report at their last dinner, "We've just discovered that fifteen out of sixteen of us are the primary breadwinner in our families. That's way more than a majority of us here. We are in the midst of an interesting reversal of roles, but we didn't realize it until tonight."

> As women realize they are money makers and major family keepers, their perspective shifts to one of serious attention and honor for their work.

The context of how important their roles had become in sustaining the family, being providers and guarantors of their family's quality of life, sank in. "I thought I was the only one, a fluke," said Sandy, "so I've laid low. But we are essentials, not add-ons, to the family and, really, to our companies."

Putting your worth in context is a real scene shifter. It will affect everyone around you and strengthen your ability to demand a raise, a promotion, a fair return for your work.

Money Changes When You Change

The influence of money on how you feel about yourself depends on which part of your career cycle you are in. Over time I experienced significant changes in perspective on why I worked and the role played by money.

Self-Sufficiency

Given my family history, I had an overriding need to provide for myself, to be financially secure in my early work years.

Emotional Sufficiency

When it became clear I would be able to earn a good living at Tatham, I added on the rewards of self-discovery through work *and* working for the well-being of my "family," the agency, which significantly broadened my ideas on why I worked.

Mighty Tasks

Ogilvy represented a test of personal capacity as well as a higher level of compensation and recognition. I was not working to prove to the outside world that I could pull off the turnaround. Rather, it was my private challenge to put all I had learned to use in a mighty task.

Serving

Going to work in the government introduced me to a totally new reason for working. I went to work for Colin Powell and the U.S. State Department because my country, which had never called on me to make any sacrifices, asked me to serve. As it happened, this also became the steepest learning curve of my life.

Knowing where you are and what you want out of work is your primary locater, your GPS. It is a great advantage to see the big picture, even as you nearly drown in the day-to-day, because such a vantage point will positively affect and inform your actions.

> If you separate your work experiences into key periods, you will find natural divides in what you wanted out of each period.

Poet Rainer Maria Rilke provokes us into thinking about where we are: "From a boat, you are shore. / From the shore, a boat." If you see yourself as a boat, you are moving along on the water. What matters to you is the pace, the weather, your relationships; you focus on your passengers and your destination. If you see yourself as shore, your boundaries matter most, for they hold and support the current of work, and you are a guide to the flow of activity. Boat looks at shore as only a channel; shore looks at boat as travelers to be directed. Whether you are boat or shore is a matter of your perspective. Knowing where you are will help you make good judgments because you keep all of it . . . in context.

We can further heed Rilke's alert to check our perspective by defining our current work cycle in a more original way.

The Ultimate Context: Work Life Cycles

I had a hard time getting the proper context for work when I counted on various job titles and the expectations of others above me to tell me. I had bosses who reneged on their responsibility for taking charge, even though it was their job. They were indifferent, scared, or incompetent. From time to time, I was given a title but no authority to do the work. Most distressing was being treated like an alien simply because I had moved up a notch. As soon as I became a management supervisor at J. Walter Thompson, the same people who had once applauded me were scowling at me because I had not managed to deflect the clients' hostile attitude. When did that become my job? What they were asking of me felt like a sea change, but it was really only a job cycle change at work. As a manager, I had a different job to do with that grumpy client.

Eventually I made my own distinctions about what's expected of us in order to assess the unspoken expectations that arise when we move to another position. Relationships as well as the work itself will be altered, no matter what the job description reads.

I classified work into three cycles:

Doers
Managers
Leaders

Though there are many sublevels in each cycle, the way we engage with others rather than our titles separates into three big cycles:

Doers are the PRODUCERS of work.

They are worker bees or specialists in some areas.

Managers create a positive ENVIRONMENT.

Managers exist in a political, competitive universe that is concerned with relationships as much as the work; they have to directly affect the way work is received.

Leaders invent the FUTURE.

Leaders often find themselves alone, going out ahead of the crowd to see what's coming, to greet the new.

Business manuals may not agree with my sharp distinction between managers and leaders, but the blurring of these roles makes for some unhappy CEOs or division heads. There's a time to lead and a time to manage; if this distinction is not recognized, a manager style will fail caught in a leading cycle.

There are differing relationship skills required by each cycle:

Doers coordinate.
Managers collaborate.
Leaders originate.

These differences are more acute when you study what behavior is expected of each:

Doers emulate others.
Managers motivate.
Leaders influence and persuade.

These are very different terms of engagement because there's not much peril in emulating when you're a doer, and as a manager, motivating others to get the work out can be a very satisfying accomplishment. But deliberately seeking to persuade others to a new cause or action as a leader is potentially disturbing and a far more demanding cycle.

There are three reasons why understanding what's required in these cycles will help you see the big picture.

One: You need to know which cycle you're in, for you can experience them all throughout your career.

Two: All day long, in any one position, you may need to follow, then manage people and projects and, more rarely, lead.

One moment we dig in and work . . . the follower.

The next, we direct and motivate . . . the manager.

Sometimes we initiate and persuade . . . the leader.

Three: No one is a leader all the time. Trying to spend all your time in the leader mode is not much better than missing it altogether.

Leadership is not a full-time role for anyone—not even CEOs or presidents. A leader initiates and then propels change forward. Change has an expiration date. No one wants to live in such flux, and no one wants the burden of leading all the time; leaders are happy to revert to managing when they can.

Cycles Affect Your Relationships

Though there are always overlapping duties, each cycle determines what others expect of you and how they rate you.

Doers

Doers engage by:

> Organizing
> Executing
> Being efficient
> Mastering the work

Job 1 for Doers:
Step Out of the Narrow Job Boundaries

Normally the doer cycle is prominent in our earlier stages of work, but we all revert to doer, digging in when we have to get on top of the new work. When I went to the State Department, I swung between doer, buried in the government lingo and mountains of briefing documents, to leader, inventing a new way to dialogue with Muslims.

The doer specialist is known for her mastery of complex work. You see such specialists in law and science, but this can lead to great frustration. But in special cases, doers become experts. That cycle can last a long time. Companies tend to lock in their specialists, pay them well, and keep them in gilded cages.

Sam of the clan was expressing that frustration when she portrayed herself as a brain in a jar. The reason she put feet on that jar, her after portrait, was that she wanted to be allowed to travel from digital genius to manager, to make a broader contribution.

For Sam, the challenge was that she was paid at the manager level but she so focused on mastering the work that she faltered on the primary manager's job of creating an environment in which the best work can thrive. If brain in the jar wants to be seen as a manager, she's in danger of lacking context, looking out at the world from her exclusive but isolating jar.

Managers

Managers engage across broader endeavors and categories of people; they are more generalists than specialists. Managers essentially try to control the weather at work. They are held accountable for creating an environment in which the best work can go forward.

Managers are expected to:

Hire
Fire (sometimes the one they hired)
Collaborate widely
Motivate (often indifferent workers)
Select key tasks (and there's never time to do them all)
Direct

Job 1 for Managers:
Create a Good Environment for Good Work

To improve the work climate, managers may have to do any number of things—muffle an unfair client, make sure someone is recognized or gets a raise, and lobby higher-ups on behalf of their group and their work.

FRANCES: FROM DOER TO MANAGER

It was Frances's job to organize the annual results of her medical center so others could present them to the hospital board. She was the doer behind the scenes of each "show and tell": the content, the timing, and the agenda. Everything was set when Frances suddenly realized there was no trend information. She could imagine the painful silence when the board asked, "Where will all this be in five years?" When she reported this vulnerability to her manager, who sat on the board, he shrugged. "We've never had trend forecasts." But Frances believed it was not just a good question, it was the question, maybe even the whole point of the review.

She stepped out of the doer's narrow sphere when she picked up the phone to ask an outside organization that did trend reports. She stayed late to study the material and handed it over to her boss "just in case."

On board day, he barely mentioned the trend data, but every question went to this subject. A fascinating and useful discussion ensued. At the end, the board chairman said, "This is the best session we've had in years. We don't have all the answers, but thanks to you guys, we've finally put the right questions on the table."

"When I decided the trend data was a game changer, I had to squash the shiver of anxiety I felt at ignoring my boss," Frances admitted. "By the way, he loved the congratulations we both received. I've been trying to get invited to that meeting for years. Now I am scheduled to be a presenter."

Frances went from being a worker putting the presentation together to manager, improving the environment of the review by anticipating what would be needed, heading off a storm of likely questions about long-term trends.

Don't underestimate how seductive a doer's role is; you may want to cling to it. It's extremely gratifying to be the conqueror of the work. I have heard many a manager refer longingly to her old job; the one she knew how to do because it wasn't as laced with unruly relationships, like managing the difficult or disagreeable client or situation.

Leaders

Leading is a cycle of choosing managers, judging people, and initiating disruptive changes. It's going on ahead, alone. Many a manager who was asked to initiate abrupt change, to step out and lead, preferred instead to stay tucked in their bunker.

Leaders engage by:

Selecting managers
Setting standards
Persuading
Originating
Changing

Job 1 for Leaders: Go Toward the Future, Alone

There appears to be only a subtle distinction between the manager's job of collaborating with other power bases and motivating the troops versus the leader's role of compelling and persuading others. In fact, there is a huge difference. If you cannot be forceful enough to change a wrong situation, then you have failed that moment of leading.

Missed the Lead

The division of public diplomacy and public affairs in the U.S. government used to be a freestanding unit of great power and reach—the United States Information Agency (USIA). When I came to head it,

USIA had been transferred to the State Department for some two years, and I quickly realized that our charter, to create mutual understanding with foreign countries, had been diminished and spread thin in its new home at State. Our desire to speak directly to the masses in these countries naturally made the diplomats and civil service experts at State uneasy. Foreign affairs experts must concentrate on intimate and secretive dialogue with a few other elite players in their respective foreign countries. No one in this group wanted anyone taking a message directly to the people in, say, Egypt or Indonesia.

So I was overjoyed when a task force consisting of top government experts put together a brilliant white paper on the role played by our public diplomacy messages, which were really from the American people, to the peoples in foreign countries. Importantly, these experts questioned whether this function should stay in State, laying out the advantages of returning to a separate, freestanding structure. This was inspiring to me; at last, an elite group was saying that moving USIA to the State Department might have been a mistake. I went home that night feeling peaceful for the first time in months. The report offered a wise and balanced assessment, with solutions that would improve our ability to build mutual understanding, not only with country officials but with the people of foreign countries, which was the only way we would ever get a dialogue started.

Then nothing happened. Months later, when I pressed the chair of the committee, he told me, "Our job is complete; the paper is written and distributed."

I was appalled. "You mean this report is not a call to action?"

He smiled pityingly at me. "No, it's a white paper," he said. "You'll get used to it."

I never did. I was invited to testify before the Senate in 2004, after I'd left my undersecretary position, about yet another study that discussed how to make public diplomacy, especially to Muslim countries, more effective. I brought up the implications of that earlier white paper—the need to make public diplomacy a separate, freestanding entity—along with my fervent belief in the solutions it posed. But I was speaking as a private citizen; it was too little, too late. I should have tried to be persuasive when I had clout as an undersecretary. I missed that moment of leadership, when I could have translated the passion I felt about the report into concrete change. I had the same excuse you do: I was busy managing the thousands of pieces of paper and people and didn't see that moment of leading pass me by.

There's a direct connection between the cycles of your work and your portrait. A large enough portrait will allow room for all three cycles: doer, manager, leader.

PAULINE JUMPS A CYCLE

Pauline is the driver, the woman you met who could never tolerate being a passenger. There was a lot of tough love in her family home. "It's your career. You make the calls" and "I never ask for answers that will be problems." Pauline was taught to be drama averse and saw herself as someone who liked to stay on the move. Her own trait was "What's next?" When she integrated all this, her first portrait was a general in full uniform and medals.

Not until Pauline studied the manager-leader cycles did it hit her: "A general is a manager. He has to have followers. There's all this focus on collaborating with divisions and directing others. Here's how I am going to separate out myself now and in the future."

From *Pauline:* (Manager)-General
    decisive director, take the hill.
To *Pauline:* (Leader)-Explorer
    originate explorations, discover new territories.

"My new portrait has to be Marco Polo. He has a great uniform too, but he's dressed for discovery."

Pauline was such a general that her people wouldn't make a decision without her. "I didn't see that was a problem until I wanted to go off adventuring in my more daring Marco Polo role and there they were, frozen. I needed to encourage them to move out on their own so I can activate a more frontier role for myself. This is not going to be easy."

Pauline set up a portrait presentation meeting, as she called it, with the top manager of her law firm, headquartered in Amsterdam. It didn't go well, she felt. Mark was happy with Pauline as his general. He used to be a Marine, and he didn't like the prospect of Pauline stepping out of formation.

Pauline began to feel that her desire to change people's expectations of her was so unexpected that no one would let her switch cycles. "My team acts like they're crippled and then I still forget and take over decisions, but I have done one thing. I created a new SWAT team, one with no titles, to handle noncorporate kinds of litigation and pro bono cases I want to work on, but I'm between cycles here."

A month later, Mark the Marine sent Pauline a terse note: "I want to help you become Marco Polo." He did hear her, but he needed to think about it.

Jumping into a leader cycle is unnerving. There's no proof it will work or gain applause in the interim, and not everyone welcomes the disruption. But it's also called growth, and the disruption doesn't last forever.

One day, after pushing against a strong wind of resistance, your cycle of leading will be accepted as the new reality. Then you can go back to mastering your work as a doer or creating a great work environment as a manager.

My goal is to get you to the leader cycle, for even a day. It's important to stretch to get there because you care . . . and because you can.

Story: Yours

As this book closes, a new chapter of your story opens. If I've done this right, you are beginning your own journey to experience the pleasures and challenges of taking charge of your work life.

Nothing would please me more than to see your copy of the book dog-eared and underlined—worn from use. In my X Factor classes we had little red books for note taking, and those slender volumes were wonderfully battered from being shoved in a briefcase, dragged along to meetings, or carried on planes like a favorite blanket. Changing how you work and the way you view the world of work does not happen overnight.

All the stories and lessons in this book ultimately revolve around one concept embodied in one verb, "to know": to know yourself and to be known by others. I call this era a period of forging ahead for women. To take your rightful, bolder place, you have to know your own unique nature. Since the pace at work won't freeze while you embark on your transformation, it helps to do the first thing first—get your self-portrait under way. You'll recall I did everything possible to avoid this kind of interior excavation. But then my new job as CEO of a broken company forced me to learn more about what I was made of. We are all artful dodgers of deeper insights into what our work can teach us about who we are. If you arrive at the management level with this slate blank, you will be in trouble. How can you expect to manage people (all of whom have their own dominant traits and unique ways of working) if you've never met and mastered your own? Lay claim to who you are, including the large and the small, less grand parts. If you can stand by your own rock-bottom self-appraisal, who will be able to dictate to you what you deserve?

A common misconception is that the power you'll need to forge ahead comes from without, conferred by others. Personal power is not found in a title or a commendation. It's found in the choices we have been examining in the book. Every day at work you make choices about how to react or respond, what attitude, gesture, or words you will use. This is your power base. All your energy, emotion, and intellect, when married to action and clarity of mind, will affect and even create your work environment.

The most common mistake you'll make is forgetting to keep your own scorecard. Very little at work reinforces your ability to do this, so you will have to be vigilant. When evaluators give you an assessment, they are just guessing at who you are; they certainly are not the ones who know your potential. They can rate you and influence you, but they don't get to define you. That's your most honorable assignment: to define, every day through the way you deliver your work, the scope and nature of your inherent abilities.

Watch yourself closely, as though you had a third eye, to ready yourself to either shed or magnify the qualities that project who you want to be at work. It helps to own the right wardrobe. Shazam! You step into the office wearing your work persona. Enter as someone who wants to be brave and clear, steering her own course, careful not to be too obedient. The powers that be don't always know the best thing to do. Rather than revert to your lover or mommy roles, remember that at work you are a warrior.

Trust your first response to what seems important to you in the book. When the student is ready, the lessons arrive. What strikes you as important or useful is what matters most, regardless of my emphasis or the size of it. Allison stopped the class cold to ask me to repeat a remark I made about the connection between work and practice. I had to stop and rewind to even recall this remark. "Think of work as your chance to practice becoming your largest self." She liked the idea of practice because it's not permanent; there's permission to try again. But the big mind shift for her was the idea that work would, and should, serve to enrich her; she wasn't there just to make the company rich or achieve number one in sales. Allison passed her lesson along: "I took this idea straight home to my college-age daughter. She needs to know how to think this way about work."

Ideally what comes next for you (though in real-life situations you may need to move on both fronts simultaneously) is ramping up your presentations to be more memorable, persuasive, and above all, authentic. Not exactly a small assignment, but you can focus first on the easy parts, such as tips on more effective speaking, an occasional sally into using wit and humor, or learning to step sideways in confrontations. I have never taught a clumsy or inadequate female presenter. Women really are more articulate and at ease in communicating than men are, but we are not nearly as comfortable with trying to sway, challenge, disturb the group, deliberately shake things up. Resolving to influence and persuade others will require a degree of personal passion and a depth of caring that you are willing to express and act on. I can tell you this: it will make you feel very vulnerable. The only antidote is to believe you are after a worthwhile change and that you are likely to be the right one to lead this particular charge. It was uncomfortable and risky and backfired a time or two for me, but I lived to tell the tale. What I see on the faces of the women who have ventured out, to lead, to dare a change, to confront a mess . . . is pride.

What is being asked of you on this journey will disrupt your status quo. One very potent CEO of a large packaged goods company called to tell me the women he sent to my seminar had "all changed markedly." I did not have the nerve to ask him to count the ways because I could hear he was already uneasy. But he set up another group, so I guess he's a certified risk taker and is getting prepared for women to be in charge at his company.

Here's how to calibrate the changes you are embarking on: once the core truth of who you are is acknowledged an essential component of your self-esteem, then that truth is nonnegotiable and unchanging. You will no longer be tempted to try to change who you are to fit another's mold. However, becoming known to others will often require you to be flexible and change because your presentation must adapt to and be influenced by your audience's needs.

When I urge you to take charge, I am really talking about leadership. Leadership is a buzzword that's easy to misinterpret, but everybody wants to own some quality of leadership. Leadership is that moment when you decide to take charge; it can be found in the most menial job or at the helm. Saying exactly what you mean in the briefest way possible is leading; daring to express an unproven idea is leading; disagreeing in a high pressure meeting is *leading; staying silent or out of an issue may even be an act of leadership. Every time you are generous to anyone, you're leading; every ethical act is the height of leadership. Don't sign on to the world's more narrow view of leadership as that one lonely job at the top. Keep a journal to record not only your various discoveries but most of all, your moments of leadership. At first you'll have only a few; those few will soon grow into hundreds. This is when it becomes fun to take charge, to play on your work stage with all the strength of who you are, knowing you are devoting all that you have in a worthwhile endeavor. It's honorable to strive hard so that what you produce and who you are become known far and wide. This can be done without getting puffed up or overly focused on the success meter. Knowing how to make work work for you gives you a chance to be influential and do some good.*

It is this respect, the honor we pay to what we can be at work which is expressed by English poet Gerard Manley Hopkins in his brief, beautiful line:

"What I do is me: for that I came."

When I left Tatham Advertising, my partners gave me a pair of hand-tooled cowboy boots. One boot read "Happy" across the toe and the other "Trails." They remain one of my most prized possessions. And they've always brought me good luck. So my wish for you is, Happy Trails.

Charlotte Beers

ACKNOWLEDGMENTS

I always read the acknowledgments in a book because they are so heartfelt, so genuine. Now I know why. Book making is an uncertain and lonely process and receiving support—emotional (keep going!) and tangible (of course, I'll read it)—is like finding an oasis on an endless desert trek.

The women who attended my X Factor seminars brought such bravery and intensity to the classes that they gave irreplaceable credence and energy to my own experiences. They have become missionaries, expanding on these ideas, running their own master classes.

Linda Austin was the captain of the reading crew, and everyone who joined in as the book unfolded gave me something priceless, a wider perspective. Martin Sorrell, by asking me one small question, blew another dimension into this effort: "Why not teach the book as you write it?" Then he sent me a whole different group of challenging students. John Furr not only acted as guide but would draft the most amazing examples of book cover copy or brilliant ideas for a website, so I could learn once again what this book is for.

I think Ann Patty is not only a gifted literary editor; she's also a best friend in the making, and that woman has a great laugh. If you're lucky, the book gods send you Roger Cooper of Perseus and then give you the team of Georgina, Melanie, and Stephen, as well as art director Elizabeth. Roger has the most entrancing habit of sweeping away doubts in order to make room for high endeavors and happy expectations.

I do want to urge you on if you are considering writing a book. It takes way too long and the readership is totally uncertain, but you will reactivate a whole web of friends you've missed. It was thrilling to meet again chums from advertising, business, government, and the profs at Harvard graduate school. Many allowed me to tell "our" stories and gave the lessons more life.

My husband, Bill, endured the book gestation process, which he called "solitary confinement." But still he held me in balance by keeping the rest of our very nice life going. My daughter and close friends who can see into my heart gave me an odd but crucial kind of counsel, as I fought the system and my own inadequacies. They would remind me the book can be a means to open other doors.

I welcome those new doors.